Ernesto Nazareth Guitar Solo Anthology

MB99178

By Carlos de Lemos Almada & Flavio Henrique Medeiros

© 2010 BY MEL BAY PUBLICATIONS, INC., PACIFIC, MO 63069.
ALL RIGHTS RESERVED. INTERNATIONAL COPYRIGHT SECURED. B.M.I. MADE AND PRINTED IN U.S.A.
No part of this publication may be reproduced in whole or in part, or stored in a retrieval system, or transmitted in any form
or by any means, electronic, mechanical, photocopy, recording, or otherwise, without written permission of the publisher.

Visit us on the Web at www.melbay.com or www.billsmusicshelf.com

Introduction

One of the major difficulties in trying to arrange Ernesto Nazareth's themes for any instrument, but the piano, is to separate the melodic line from its accompaniment: both are so closely together (that is one of the strongest characteristics of his pianistic style of composition) that it becomes almost impossible to treat one of the features disregarding the other. If one did that the result would be only a pale and incomplete portrait of what was intended by the composer. That thought has guided us in the making of this book. In spite of the huge obstacles that resulted from the transposition of a piece originally written for the piano – a very rich instrument regarding the expressive recourses – to the more "modest" guitar, we always kept in mind our principal intention: to preserve at the most all the melodic dialogues of the scores, in special the ones between the melody and the bass line, both the elements that form the soul of Nazareth's compositions. We obviously had to do some changes. Thus, for instance, in some arrangements it was necessary to transpose the original key to a more apropriate one (at the guitar view-point, of course). Some phrases or fragments had also to be written an octave higher or lower (that can be perfectly understandable if we consider the very wide melodic range of the piano and the extensive way with which Nazareth uses it). Needless to say that all those recourses were used only when it has been strictly necessary.

Despite the fact that those 28 pieces are only a little portion of Nazareth's work, this group of arrangements represents a good and representative panel. Among them there are some of Nazareth's greatest hits ("Apanhei-te Cavaquinho", "Odeon", "Brejeiro", "Ameno Resedá", etc.) as well as other not so known compositions– but no less beautiful and important. Listening to those pieces one can observe the compositional talent of Nazareth and his incredible harmonic, melodic and – specially – rhythmic versatility. Each of them has its own and unmistakable personality.

The most part of the scores of this book – as well as in Nazarethian repertoire – is composed by tangos brasileiros (i.e., Brazilian tangos), but there are also some polcas and some of his most expressive valsas, like "Confidências" and "Coração que Sente".

Ernesto Nazareth was born in Rio de Janeiro in 1863. When still a boy he started to study the piano with his mother, who thought him, besides the classics, several polcas, which were then the most popular rhythm at dance parties. Thus it is not so surprising that a polca entitled "Você bem sabe", was the first composition by the 14-years-old Ernesto. After that fact his musical development went on very quickly. He soon started to play with other musicians at several rodas de choro (i.e., a kind of choro jam sessions) around the city, but he never stopped to compose Brazilian tangos, polcas and valsas. Nazareth was then a well-known name within the musical scenery of Rio, but he only became a national (and international) sucess when he was 30, with the publication of his tango "Brejeiro". In 1924, 61 years old, Ernesto tasted a new kind of experience: with an orchestra (which had, among its members, the young cellist Heitor Villa-Lobos) he started to play at Odeon theather making the musical accompaniment for soundless movie pictures. That season resulted into an important fruit: the tango "Odeon", one of his most beautiful and popular compositions. From 1923 on Nazareth's health began to go worse. A parcial deafness brought him a severe depression which caused emotional and psychological disturbs. He was finally put into two asylums, dying in the second one, on February 1st, 1934, at the age of 71. Besides having left countless compositions of extraordinary quality, Nazareth is considered one of the best pianists of popular music, having created a true Brazilian syncopated piano school which spreads from the choro to the samba and the bossa-nova.

TABLE OF CONTENTS

Introduction	2
Ameno Resedá	4
Apanhei-te Cavaquinho	6
Brejeiro	12
Confidências	16
Coração que Sente	24
Escorregando	30
Escovado	34
Faceira	39
Floraux	44
Fon-fon	50
Garoto	56
Gentes! O Imposto Pegou?	60
Gotas de Ouro	64
Labirinto	70
Matuto	74
Nenê	78
Nove de Julho	83
Odeon	88
Pingüim	92
Quebradinha	96
Rayon d'Or	100
Sagaz	104
Sarambeque	108
Saudade	112
Tango Carnavalesco	118
Tupinambá	124
Vitorioso	128
1922	132

Ameno Resedá

(polca)

Ernesto Nazareth
(arranged by Flavio Henrique Medeiros)

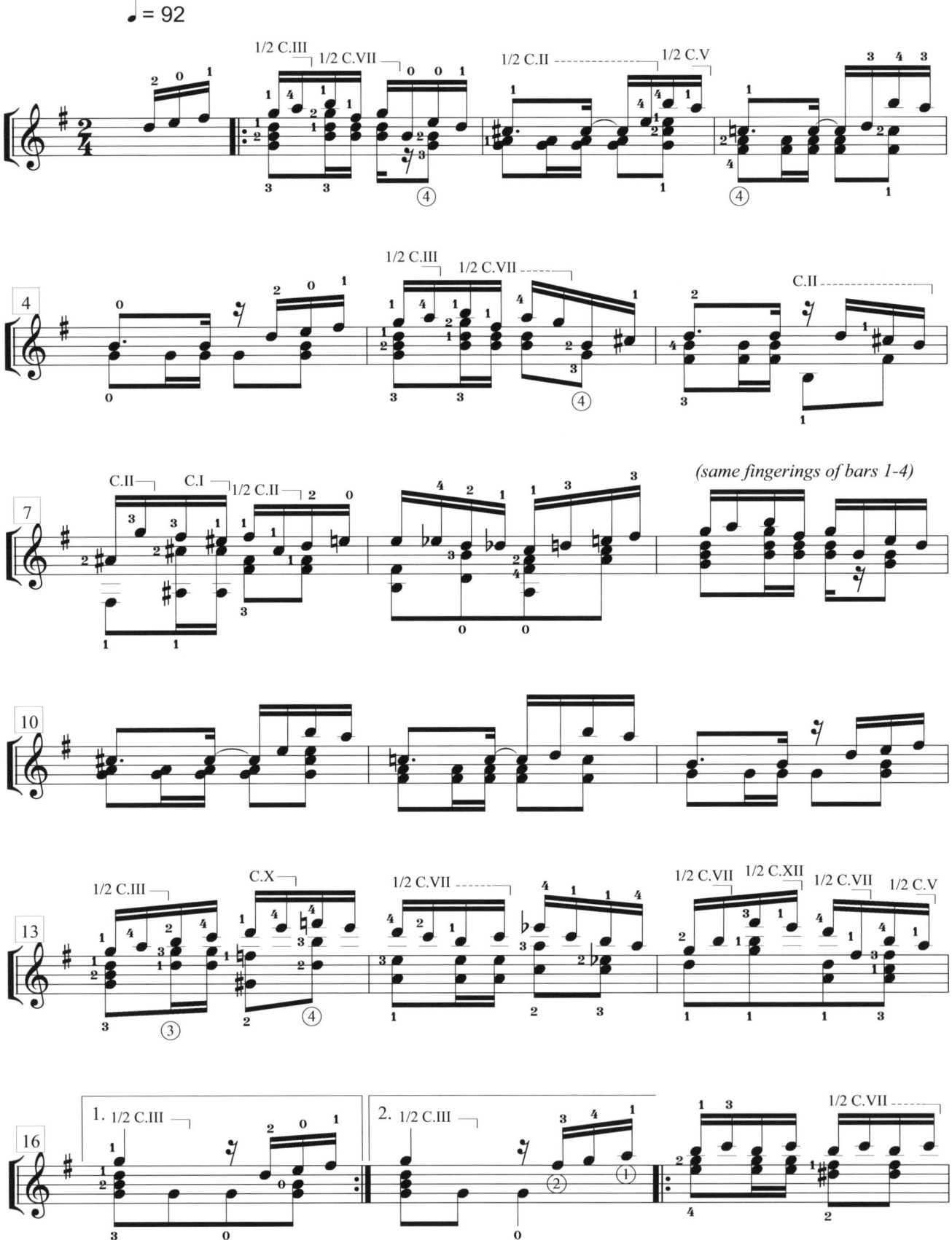

Apanhei-te Cavaquinho
(polca)

Ernesto Nazareth
(arranged by Flavio Henrique Medeiros)

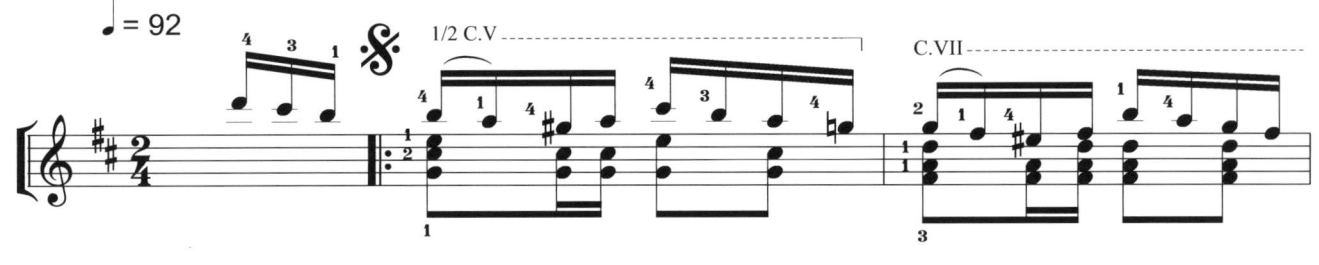
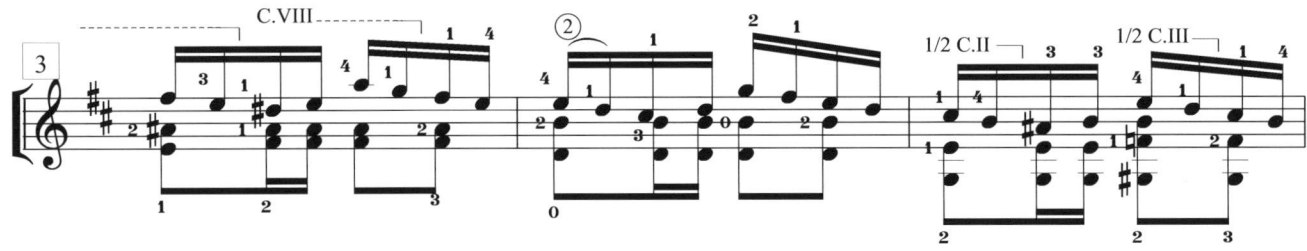
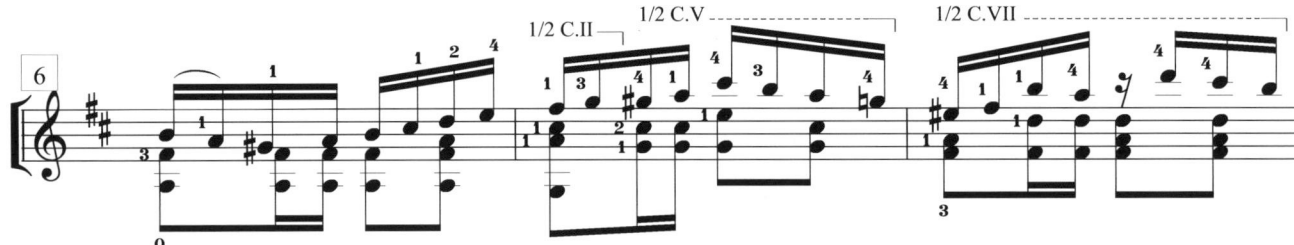

(same fingerings of bars 1-6)

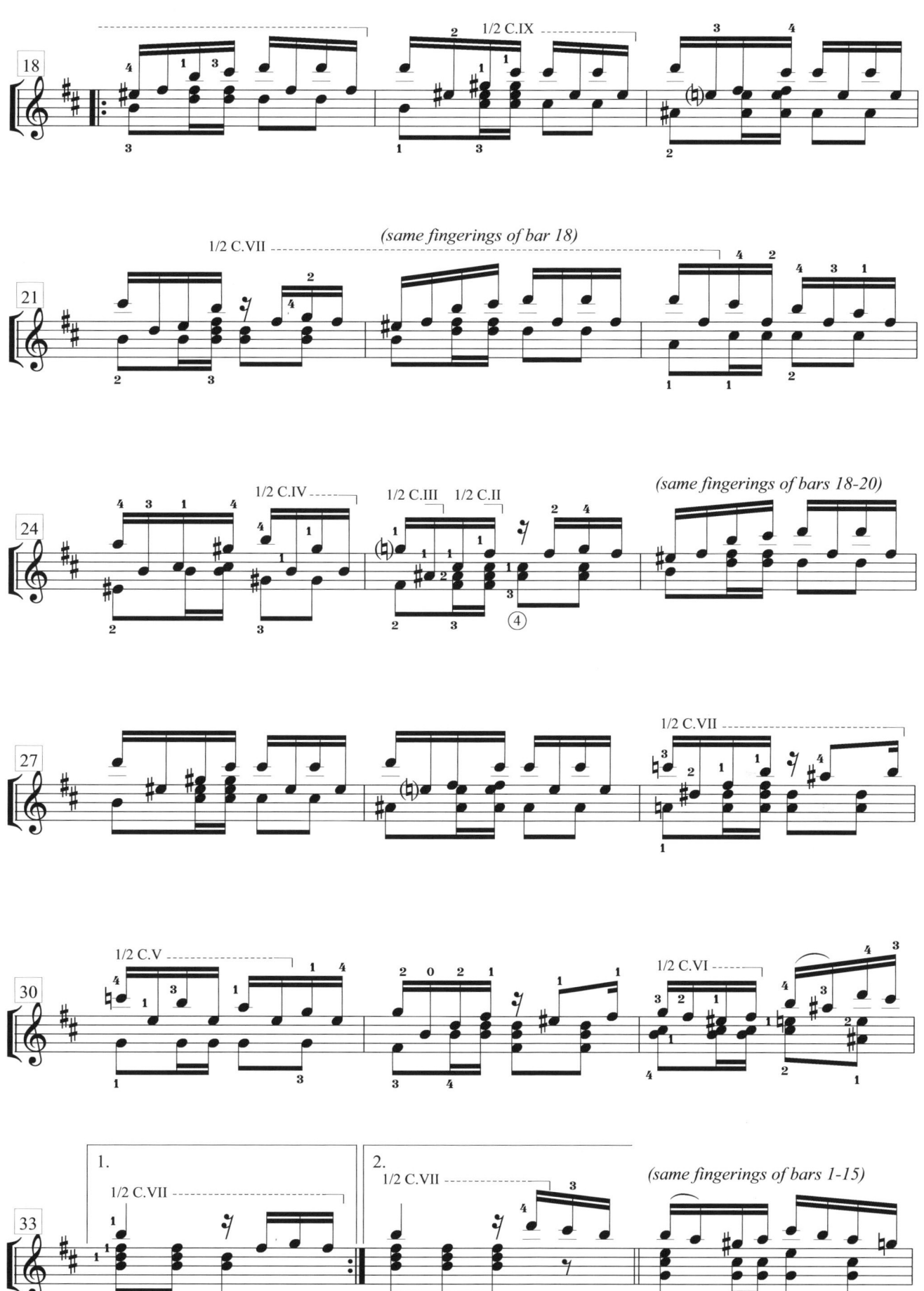

Brejeiro

(tango brasileiro)

[6th = D]

Ernesto Nazareth
(arranged by Carlos Almada)

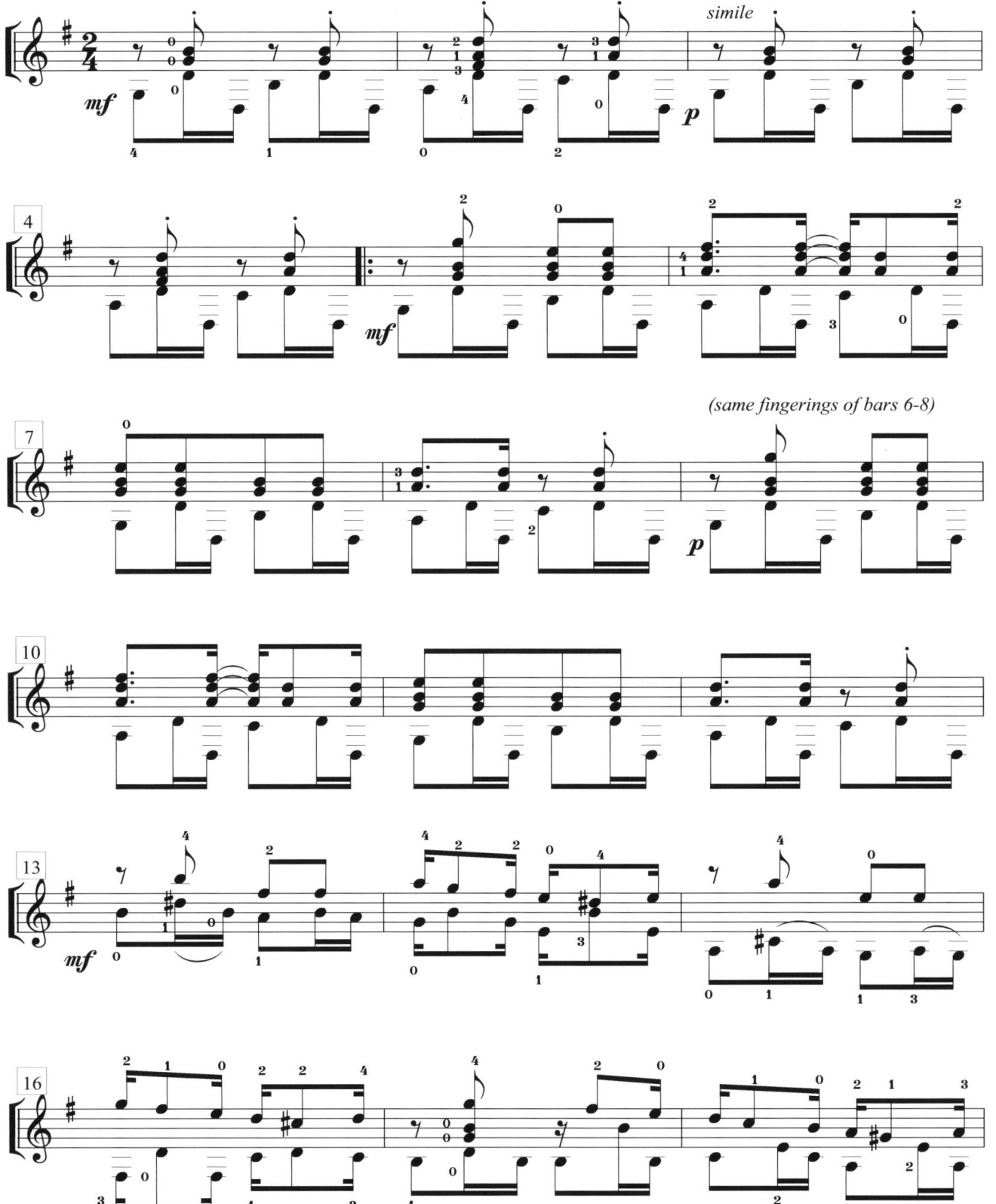

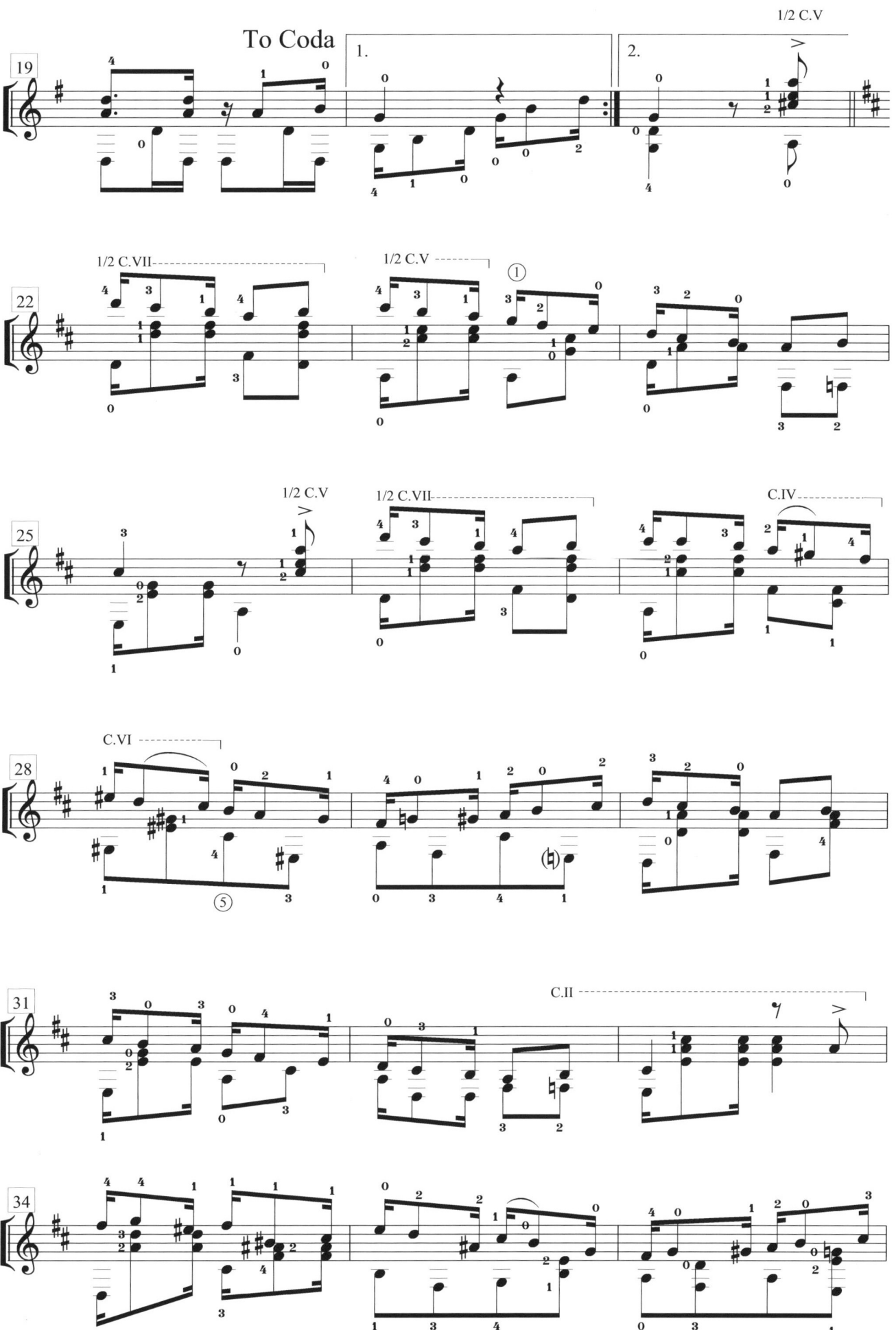

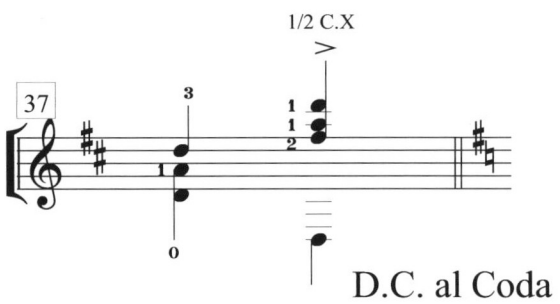

D.C. al Coda

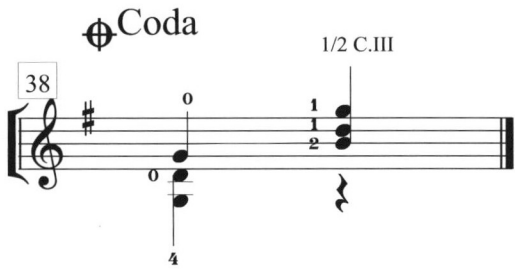

This page has been left blank
to avoid awkward page turns

Confidências
(valsa)

Ernesto Nazareth
(arranged by Flavio Henrique Medeiros)

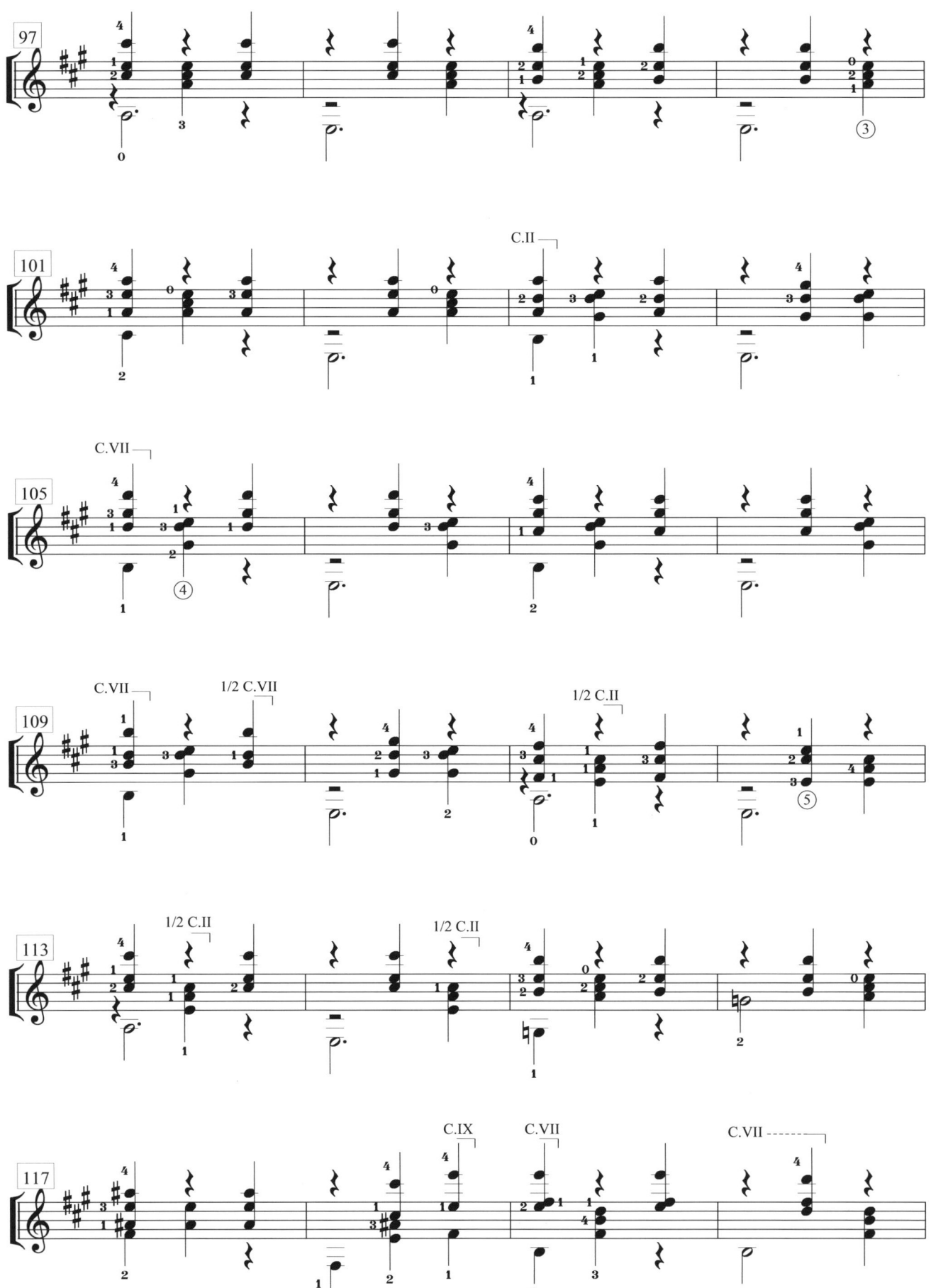

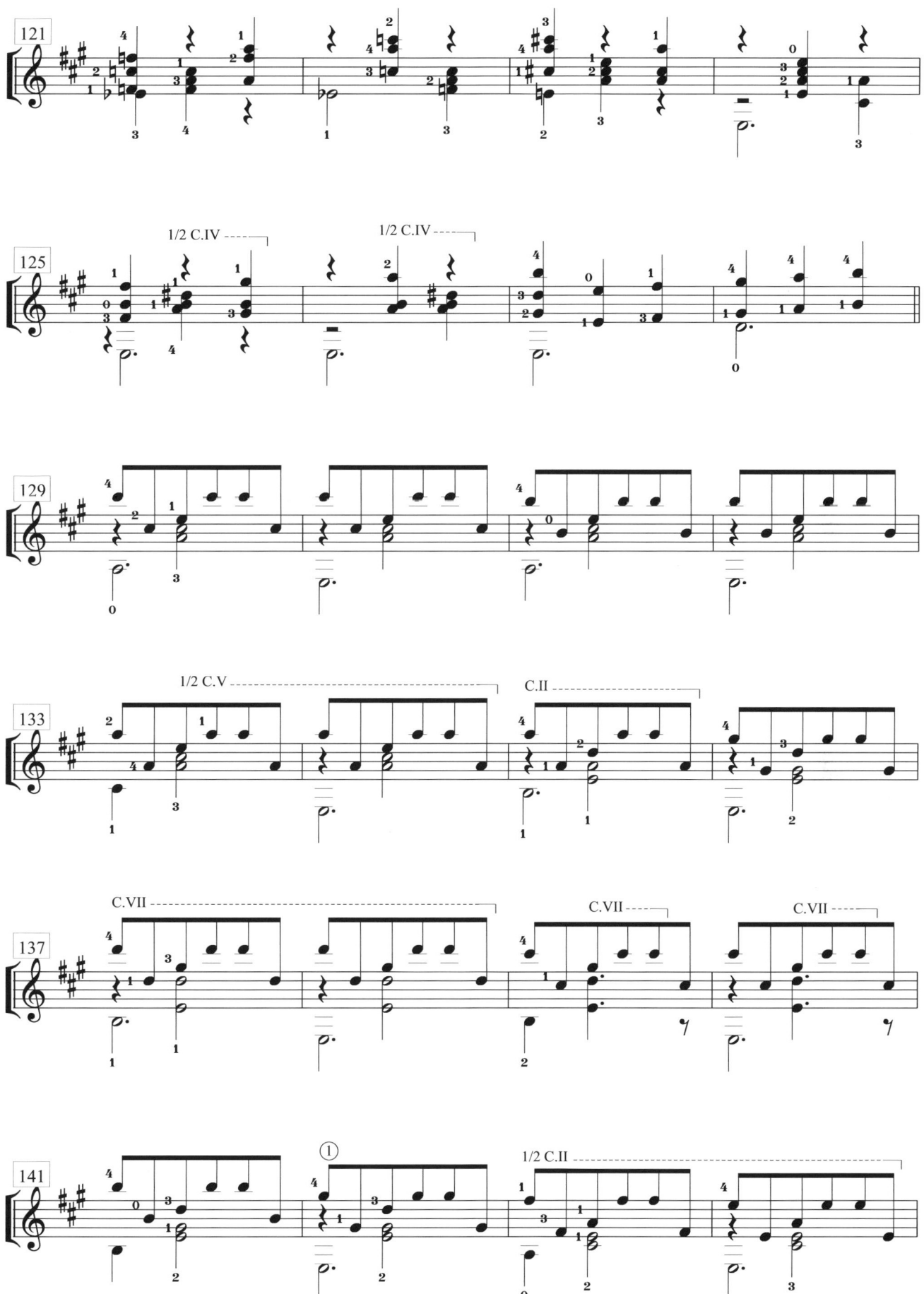

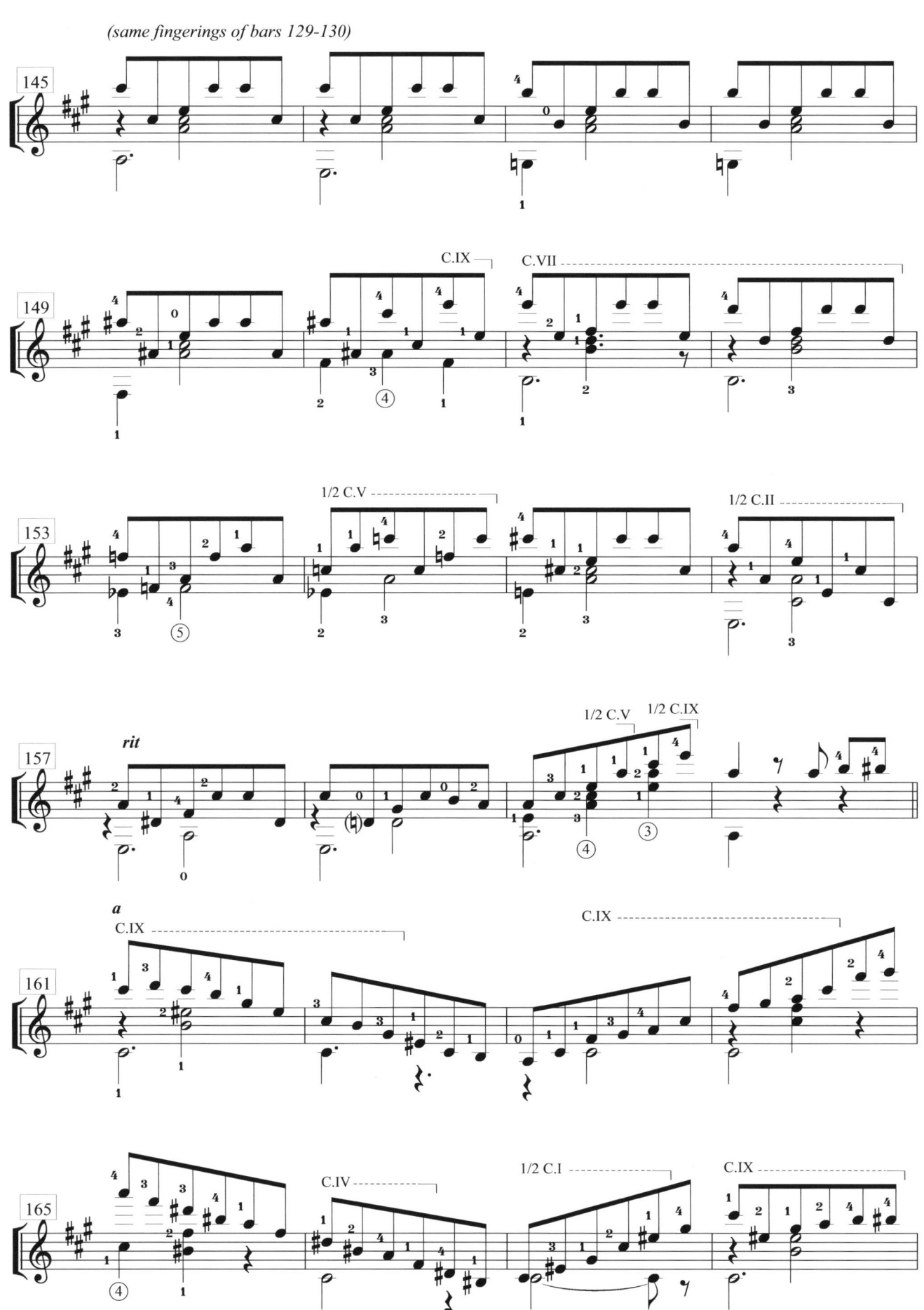

Coração que sente
(valsa)

Ernesto Nazareth
(arranged by Carlos Almada)

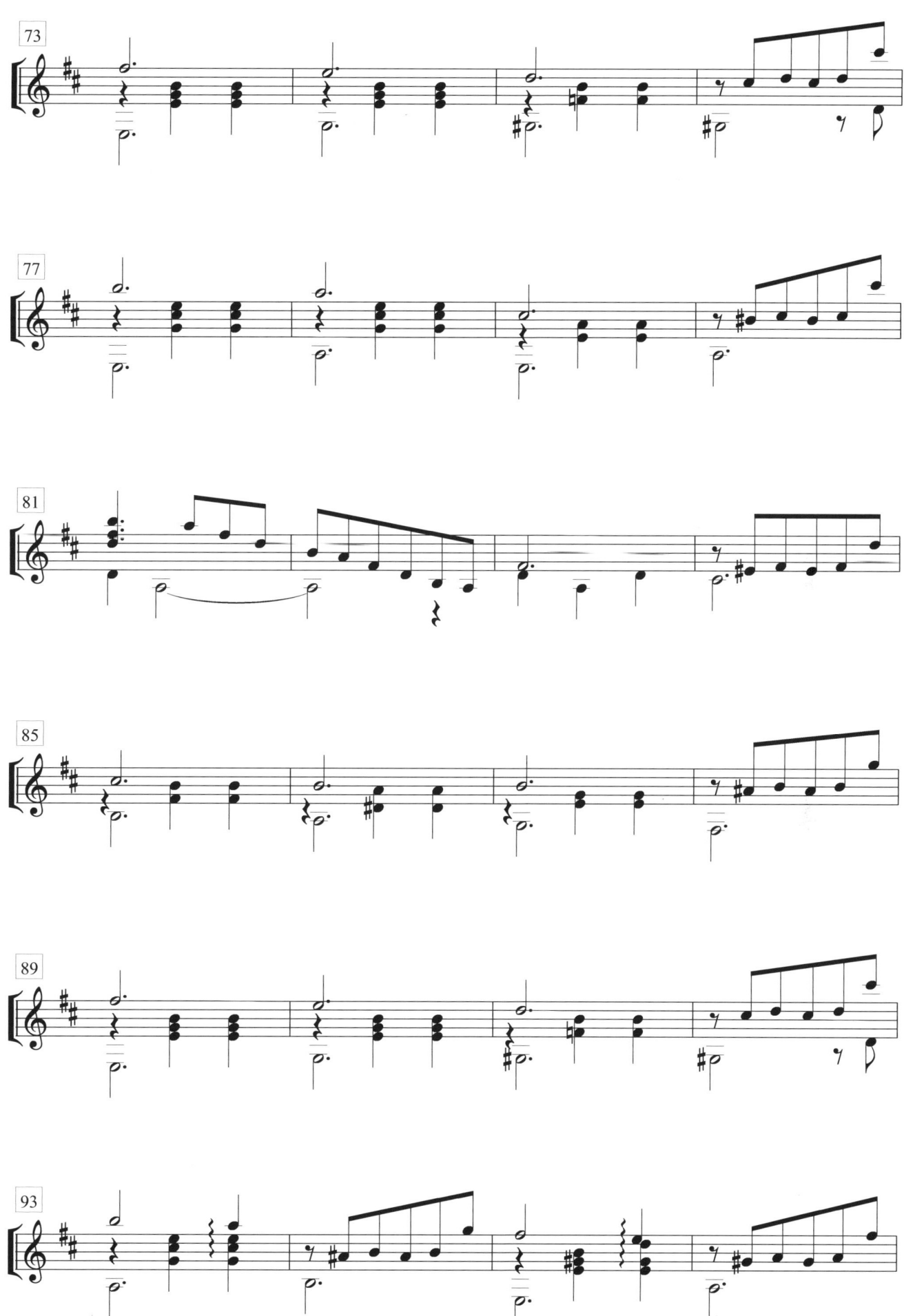

Escorregando

(tango brasileiro)

Ernesto Nazareth
(arranged by Carlos Almada)

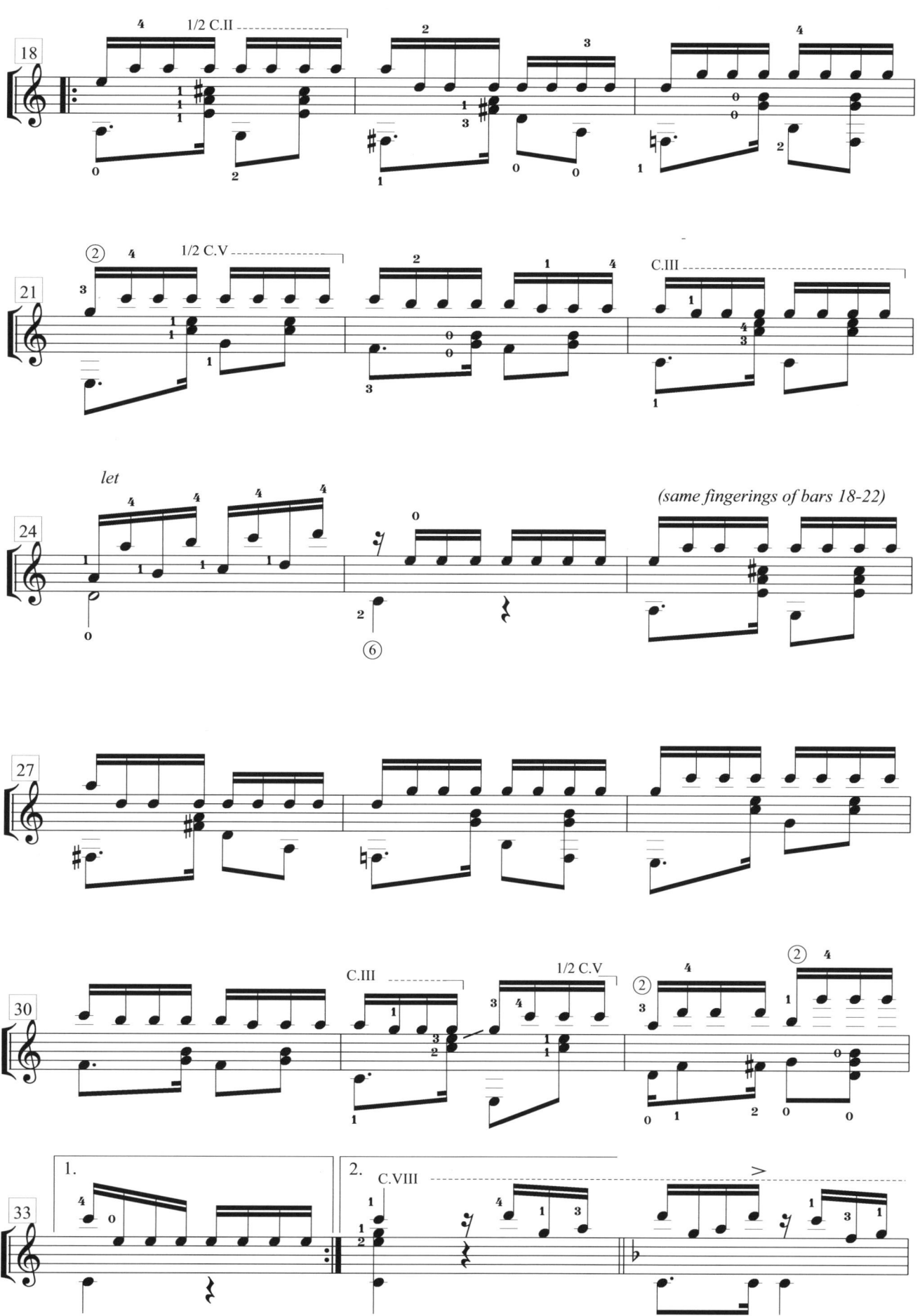

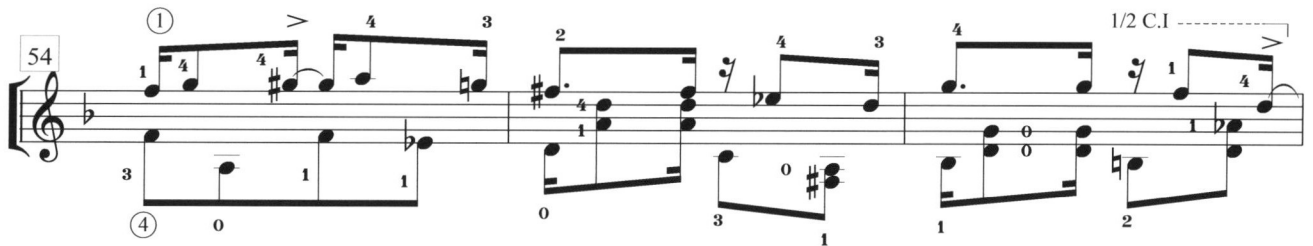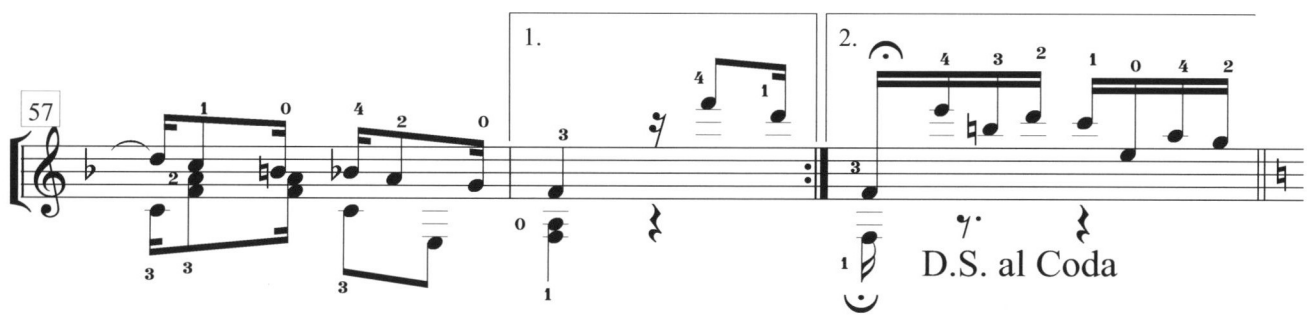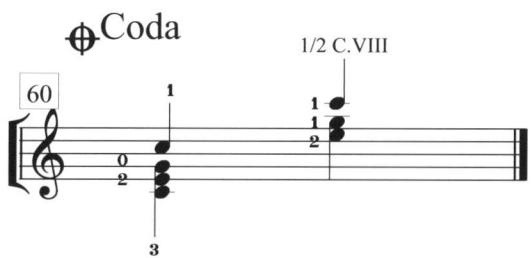

Escovado

(tango brasileiro)

Ernesto Nazareth
(arranged by Flavio Henrique Medeiros)

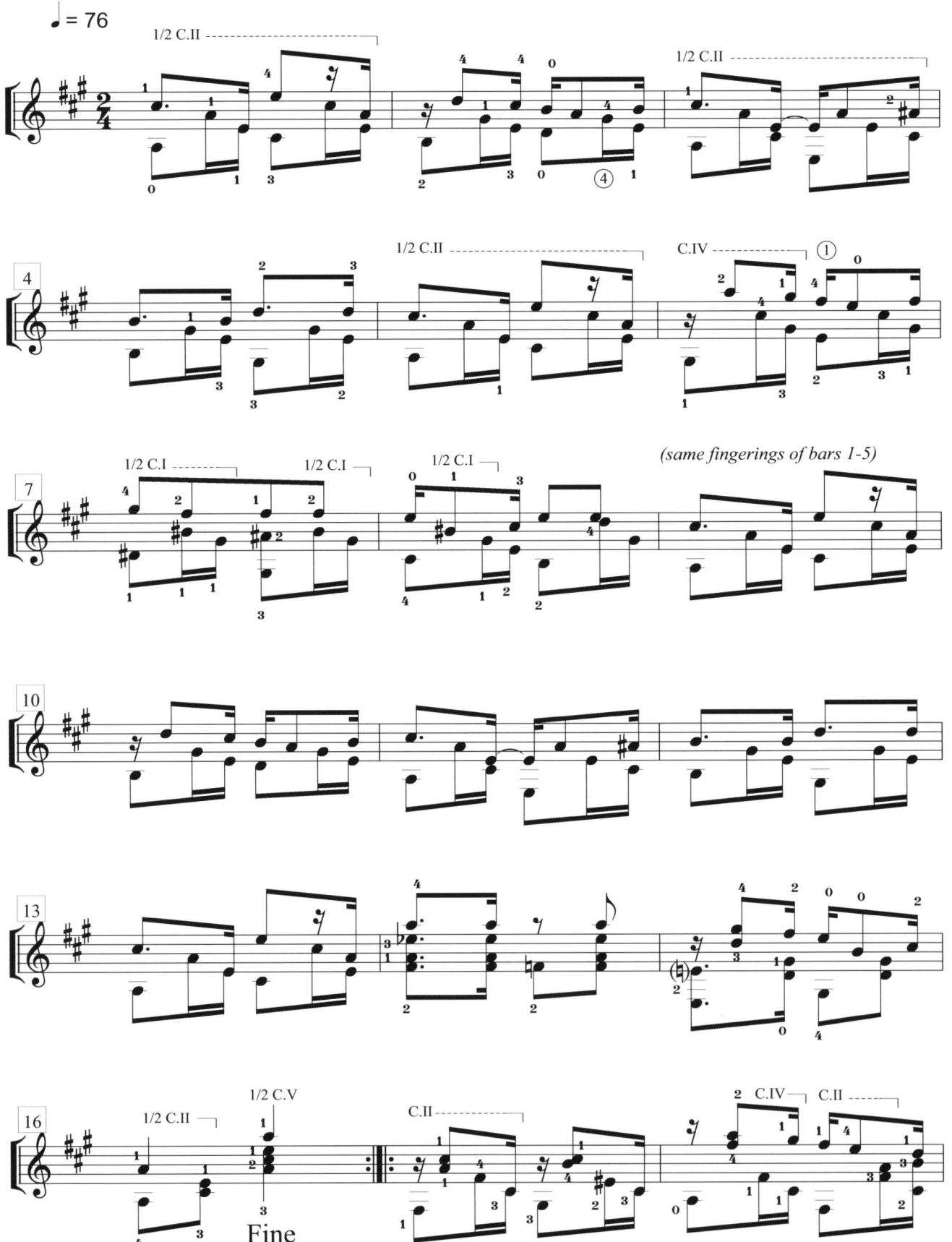

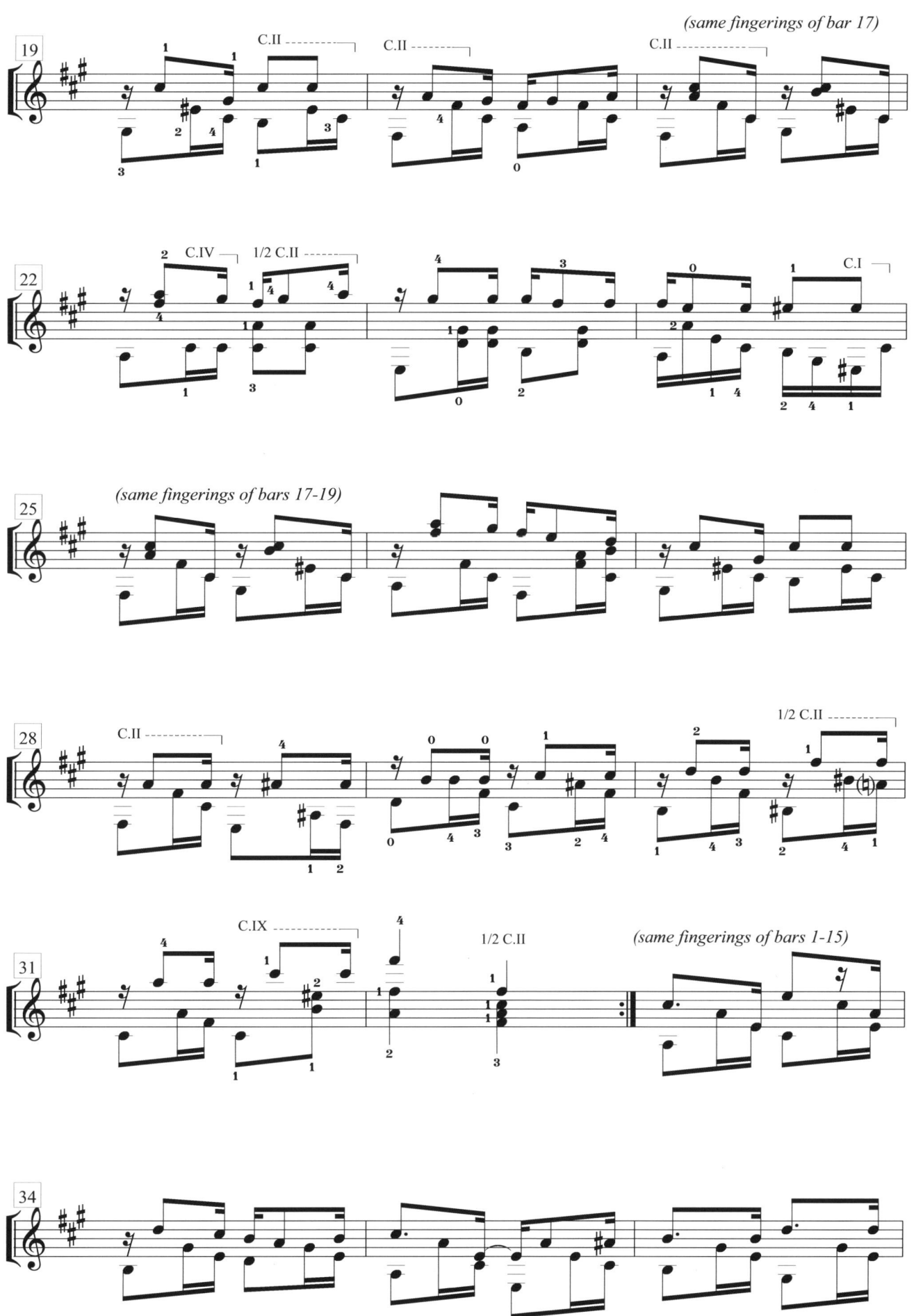

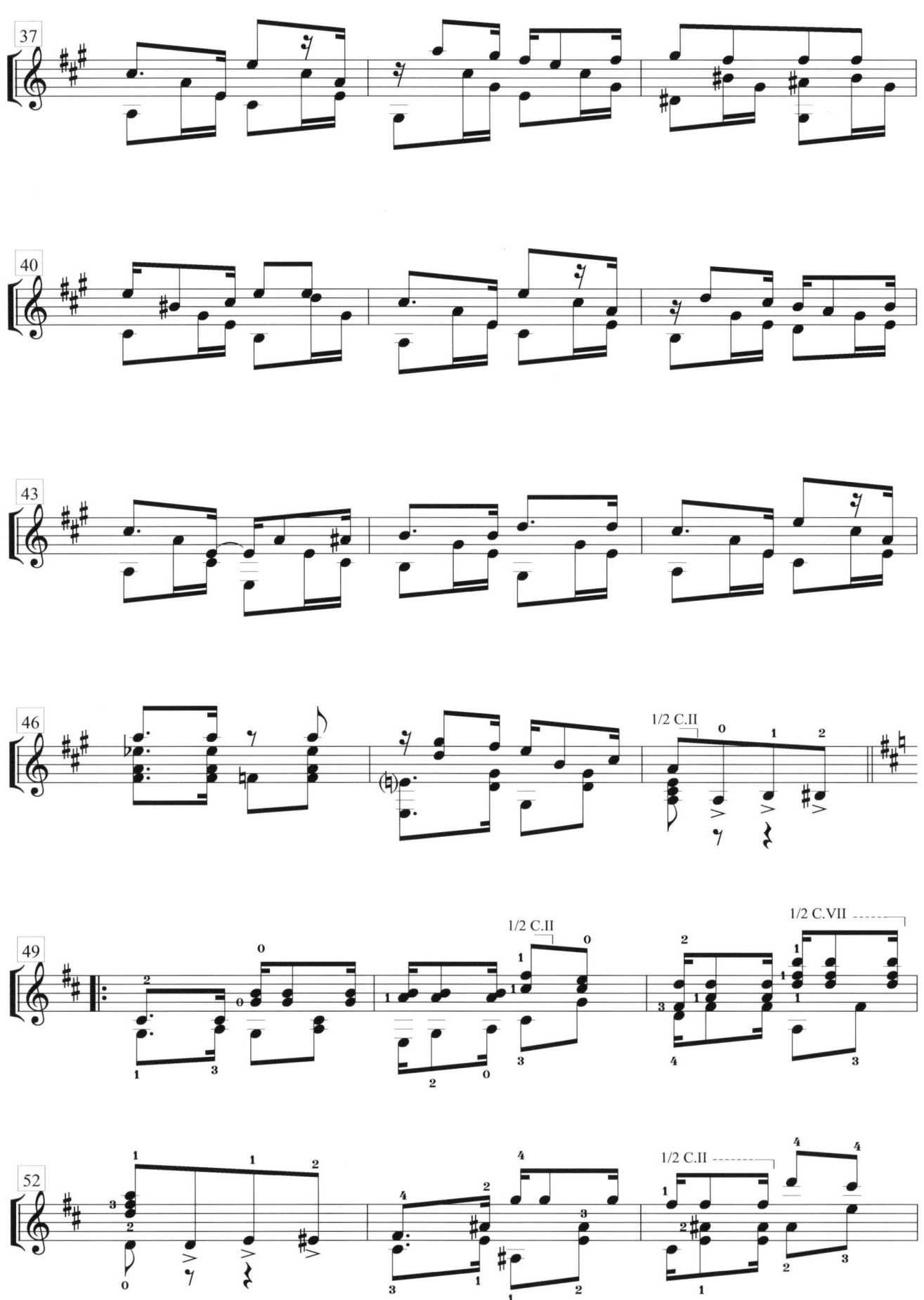

D.C. al Fine

Faceira

(valsa)

Ernesto Nazareth
(arranged by Flavio Henrique Medeiros)

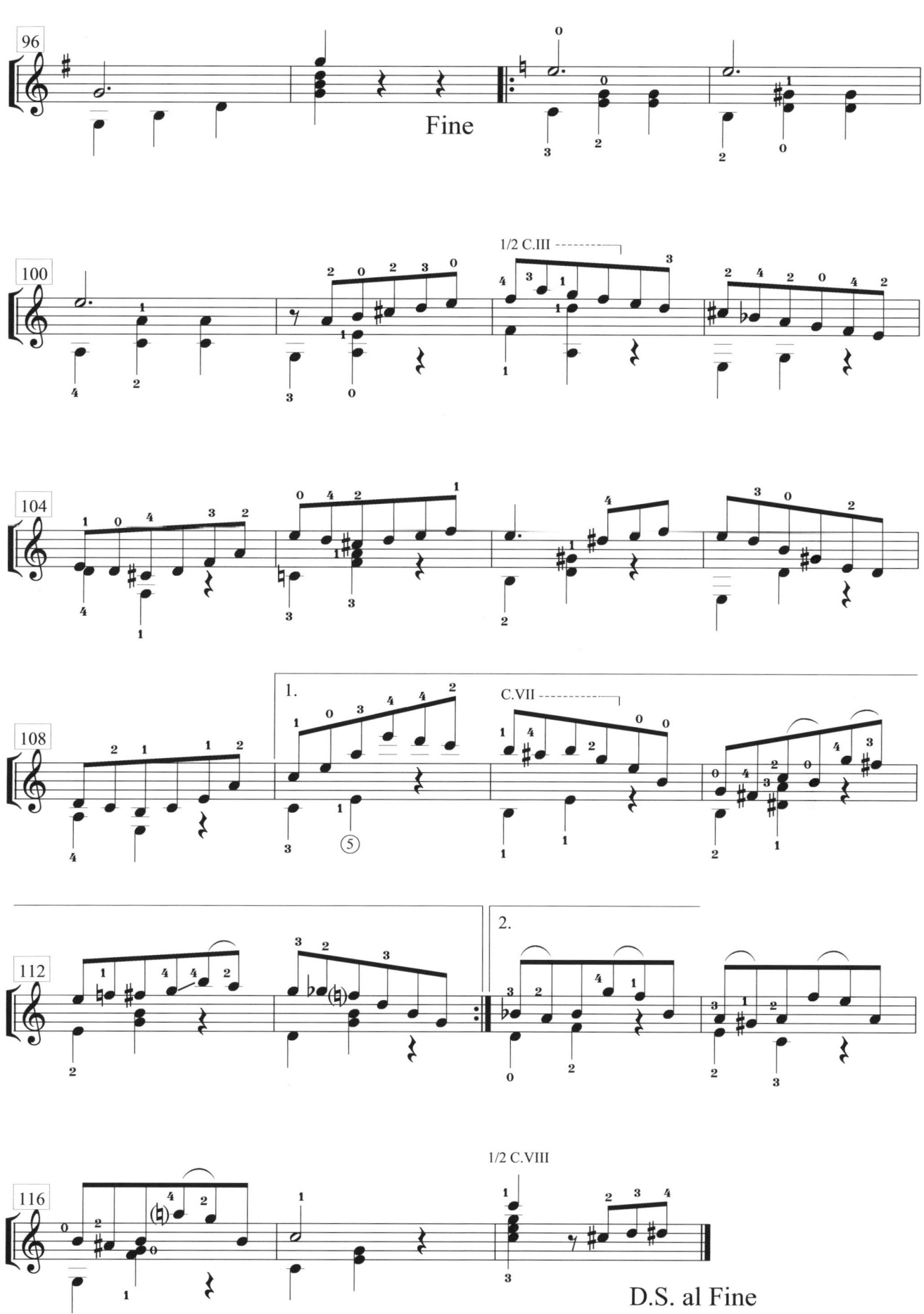

43

Floraux

(tango brasileiro)

Ernesto Nazareth
(arranged by Flavio Henrique Medeiros)

44

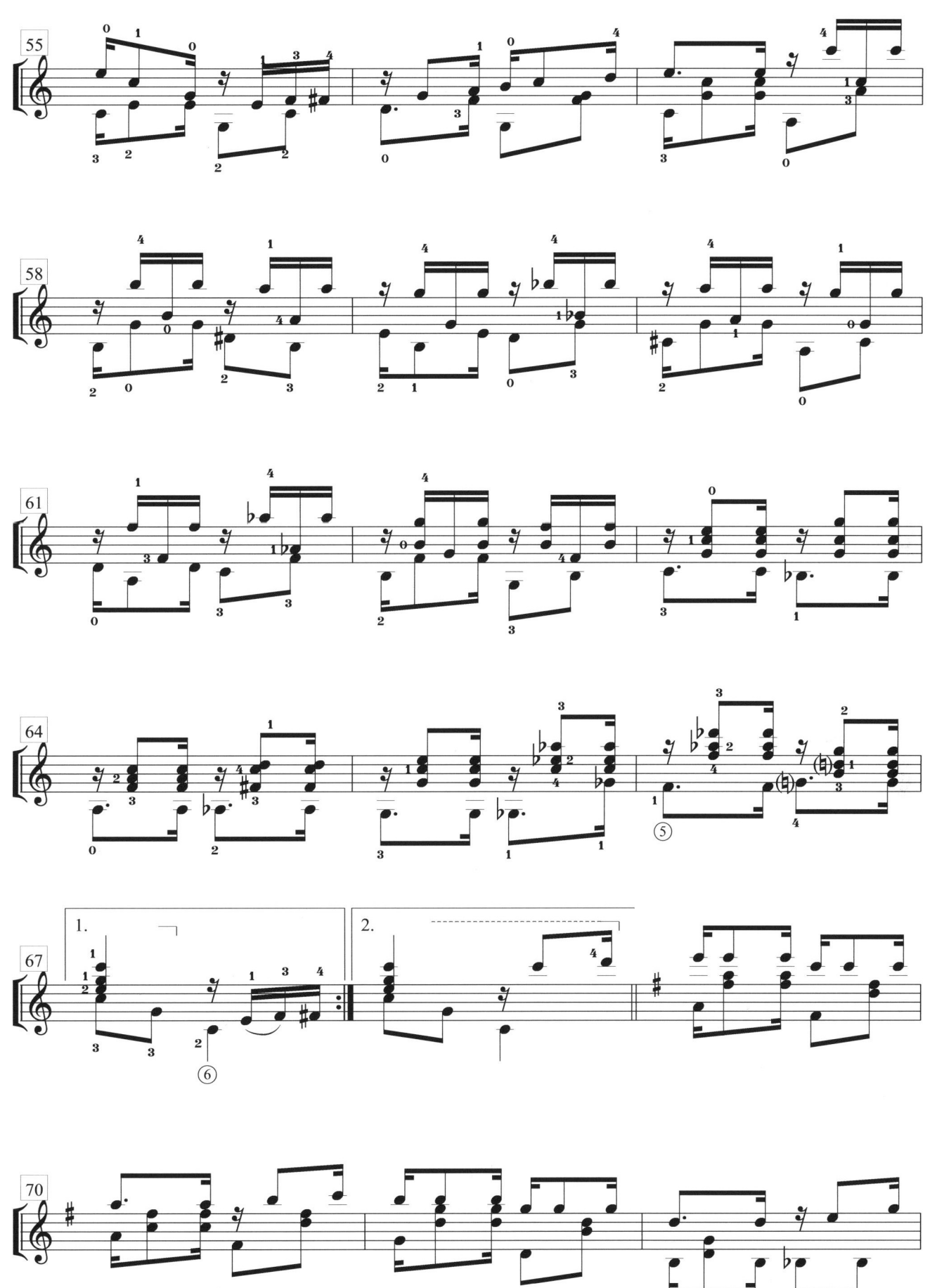

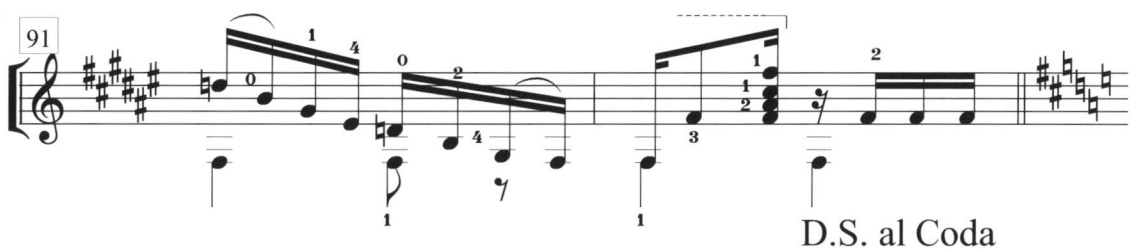

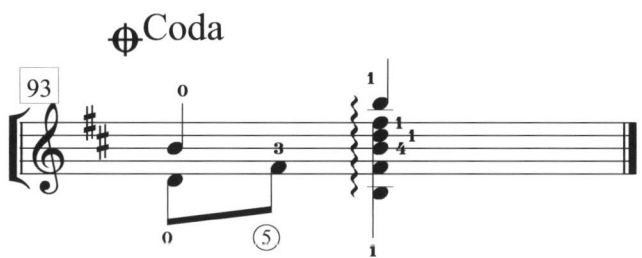

Fon-fon
(tango brasileiro)

Ernesto Nazareth
(arranged by Carlos Almada)

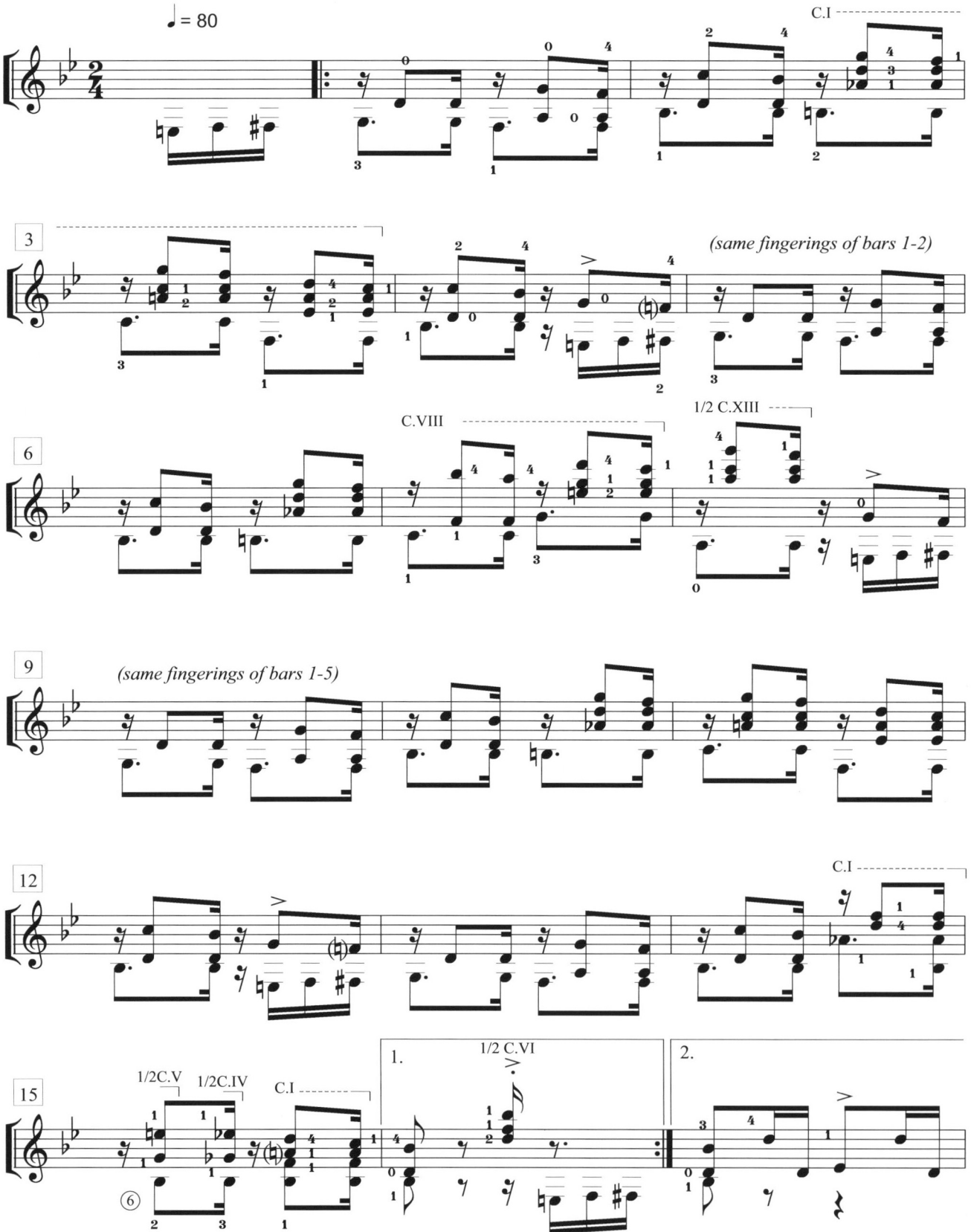

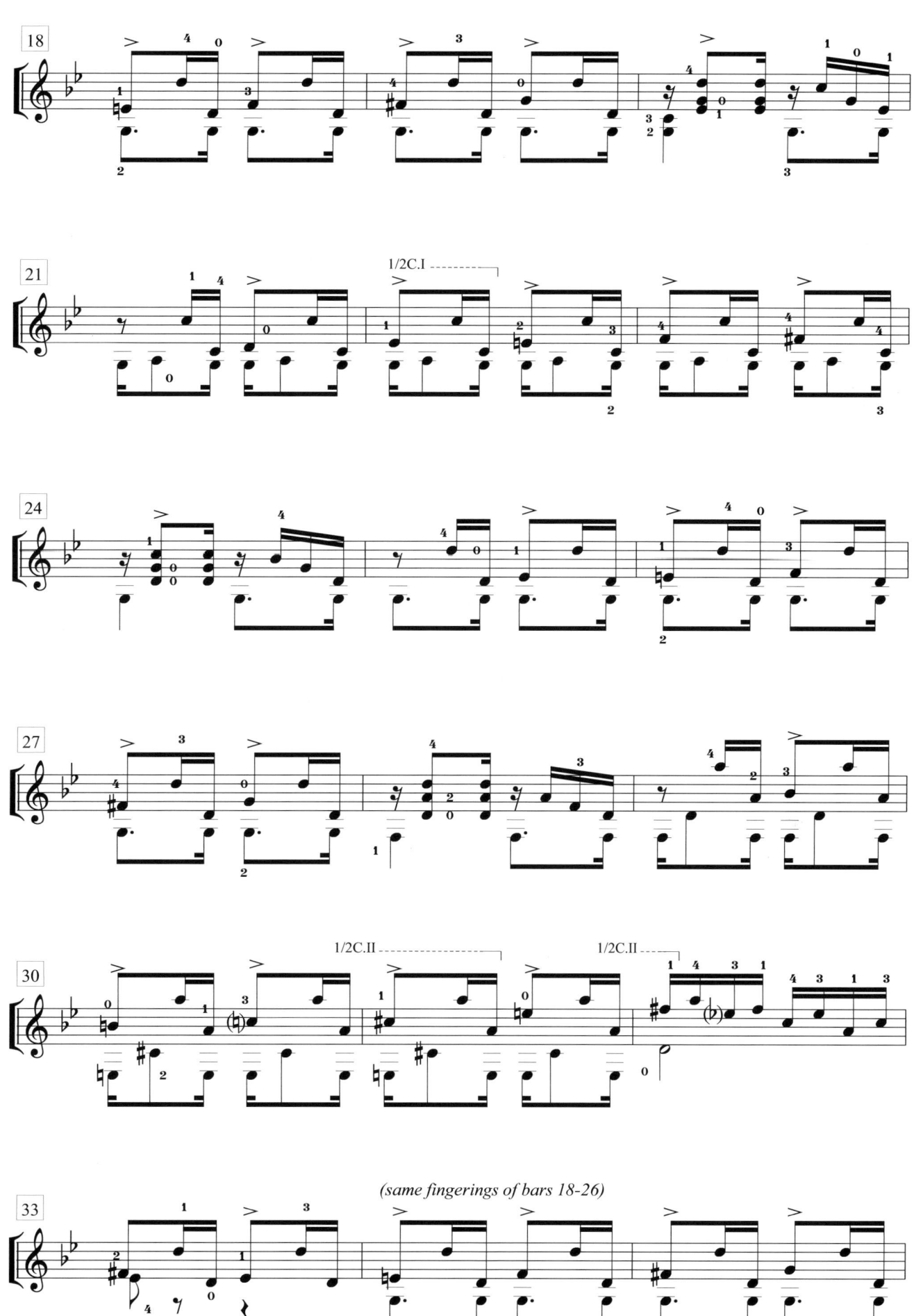
(same fingerings of bars 18-26)

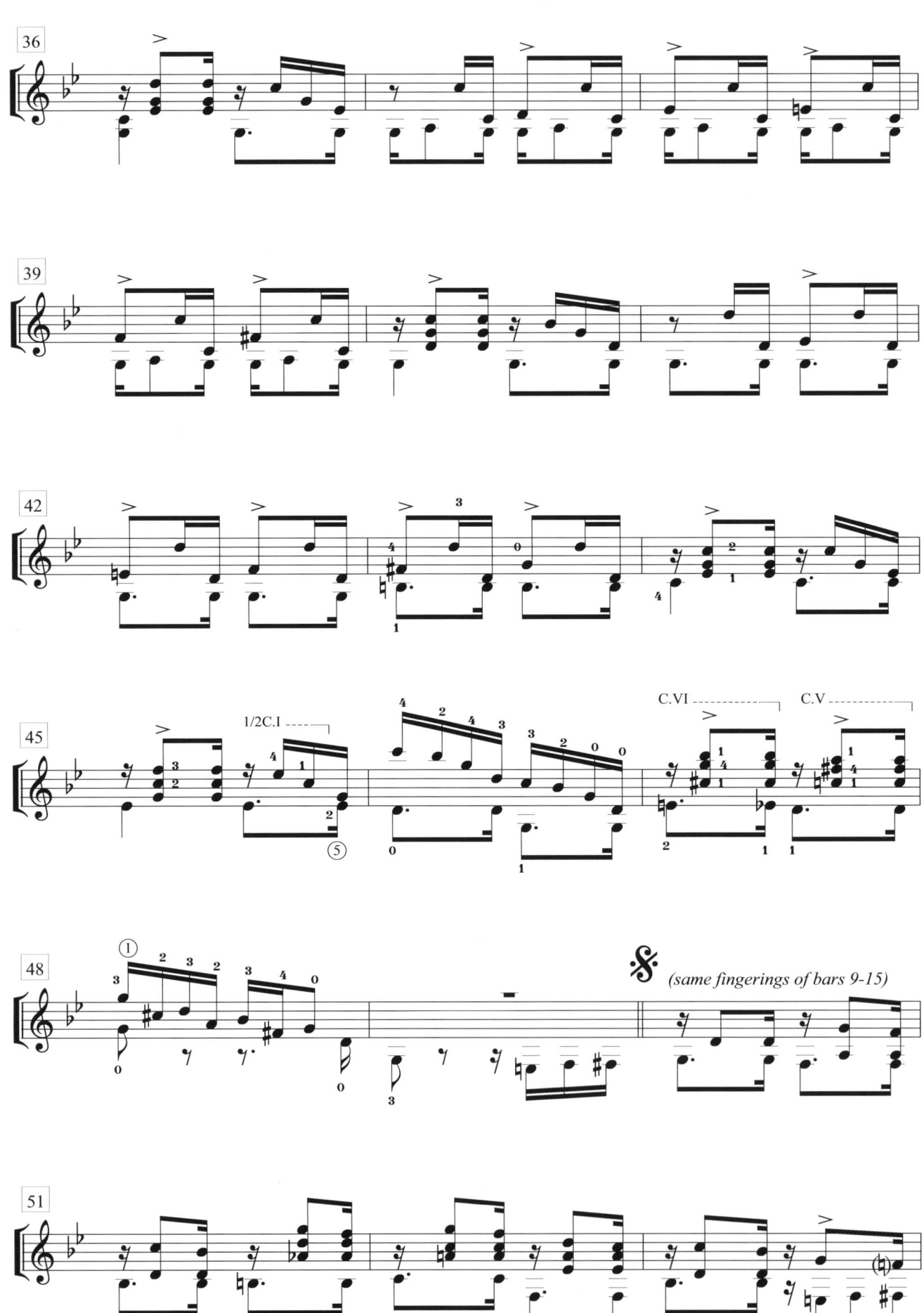

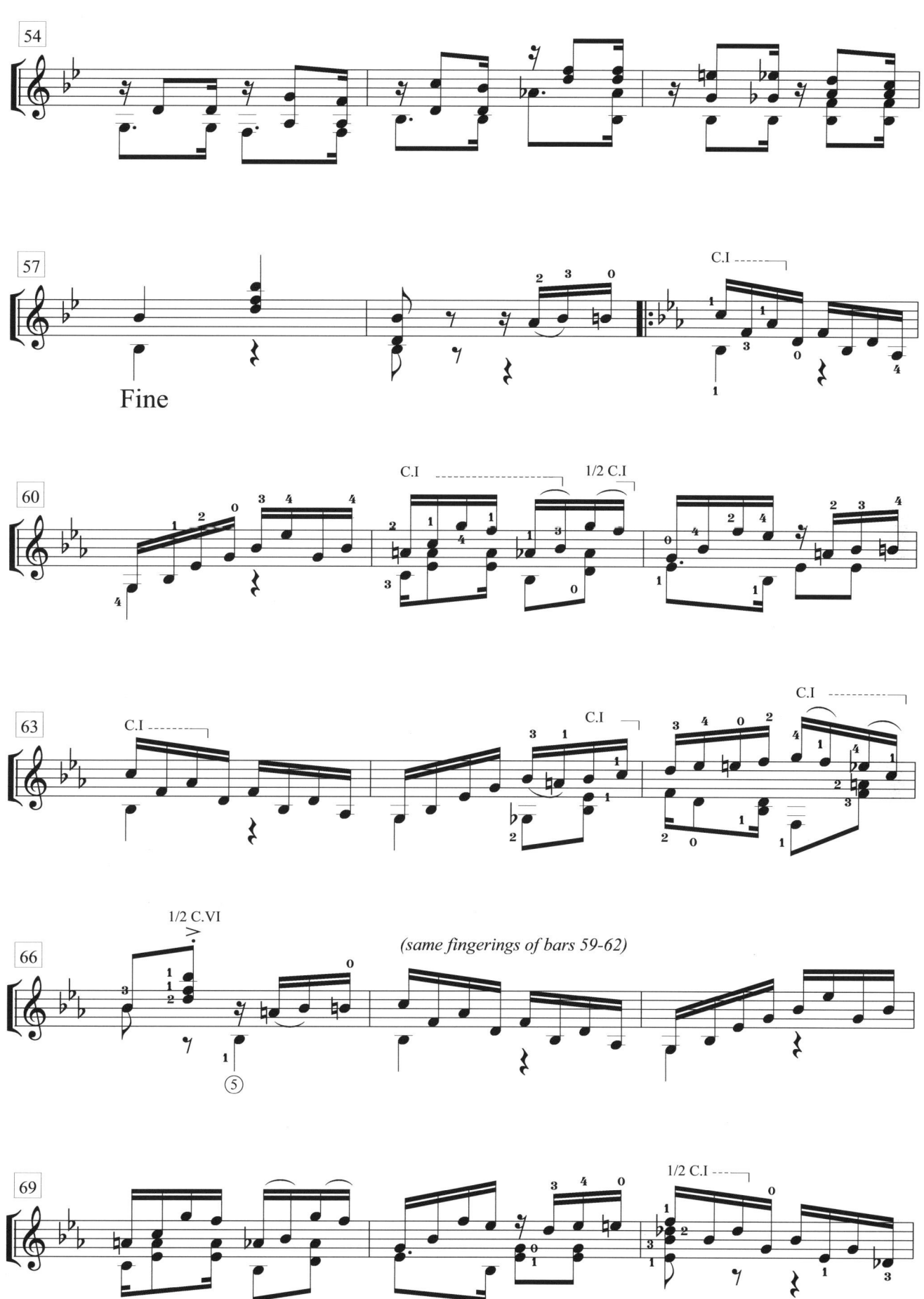

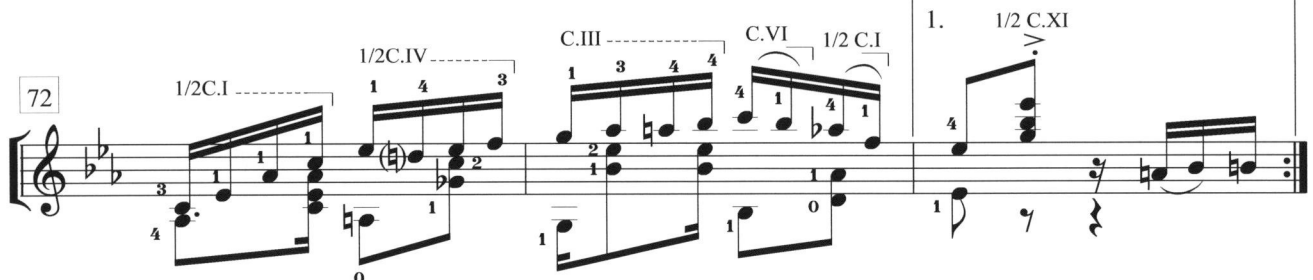
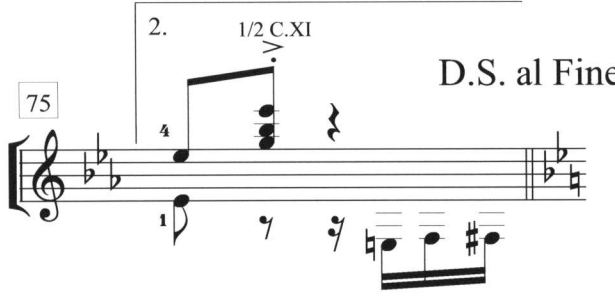

D.S. al Fine

This page has been left blank to avoid awkward page turns.

Garôto

(tango brasileiro)

Ernesto Nazareth
(arranged by Carlos Almada)

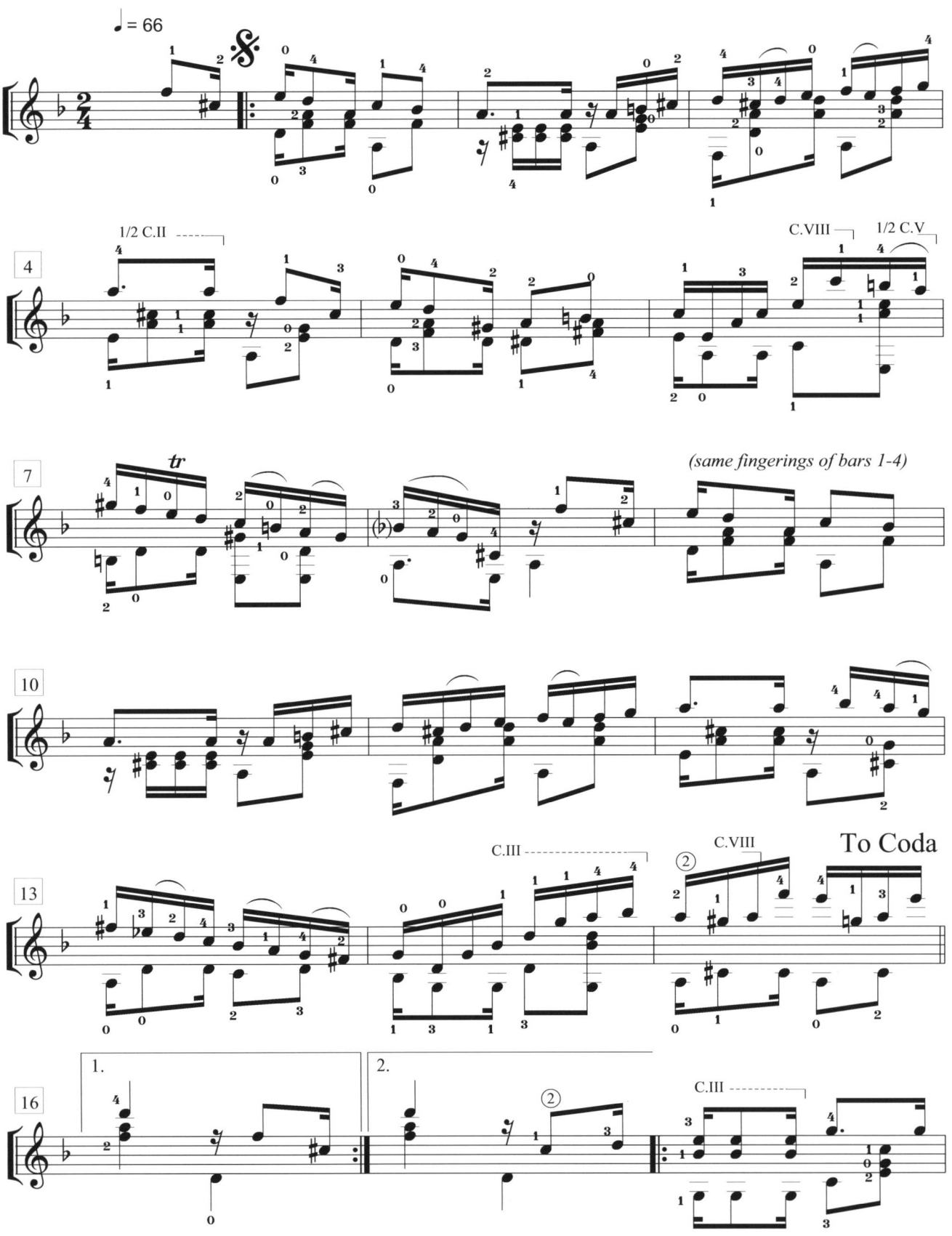

55
C.IX
58
(same fingerings of bars 51-54)
61
64
C.II
1.
1/2 C.X
2.
D.S. al Coda
Coda
68

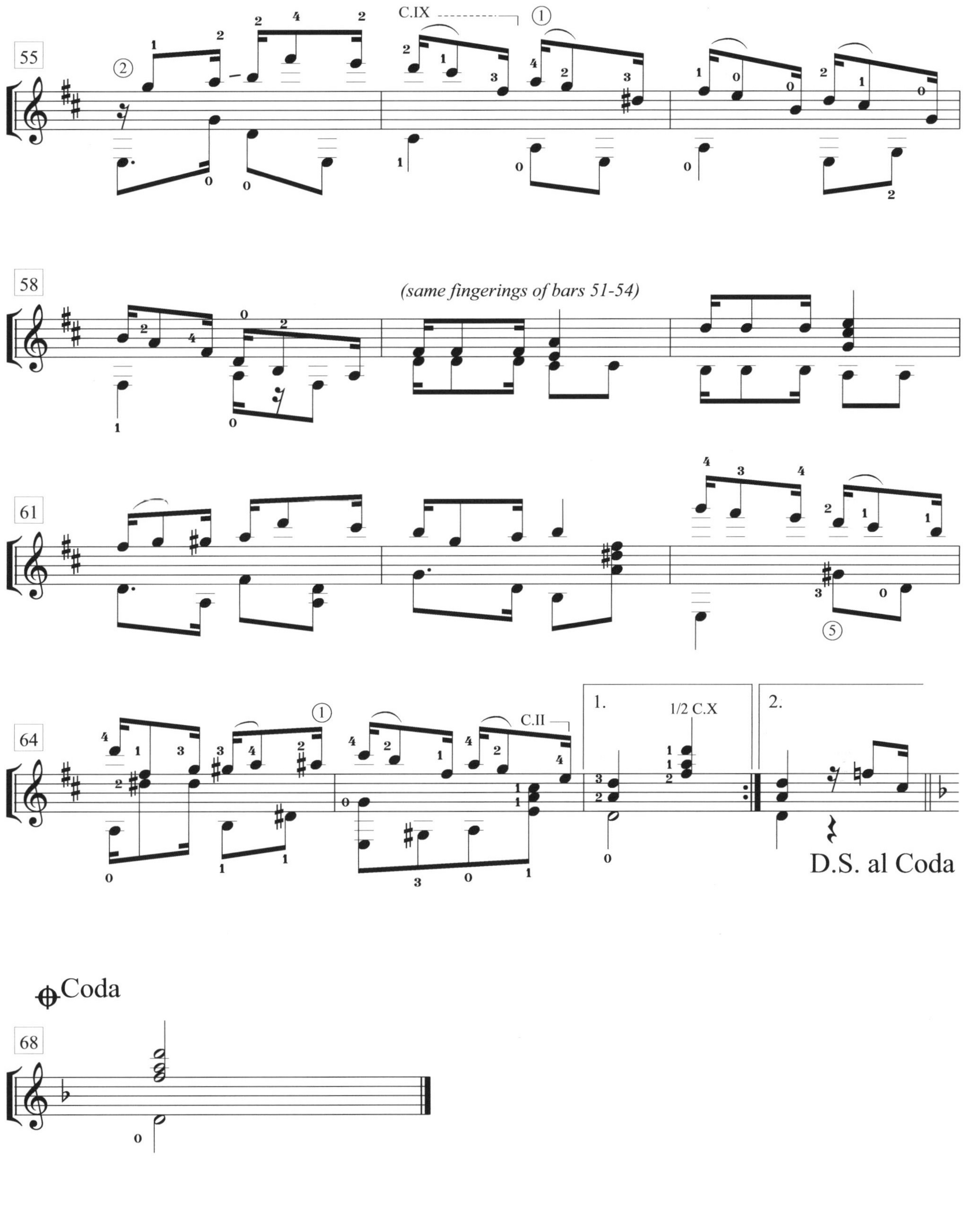

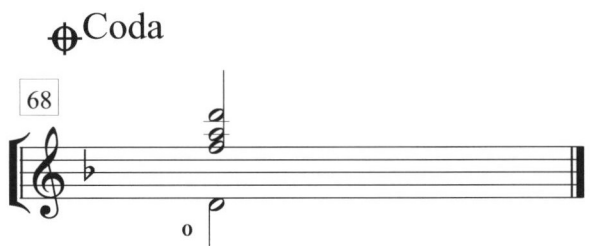

Gentes! O Imposto Pegou?
(polca)

Ernesto Nazareth
(arranged by Flavio Henrique Medeiros)

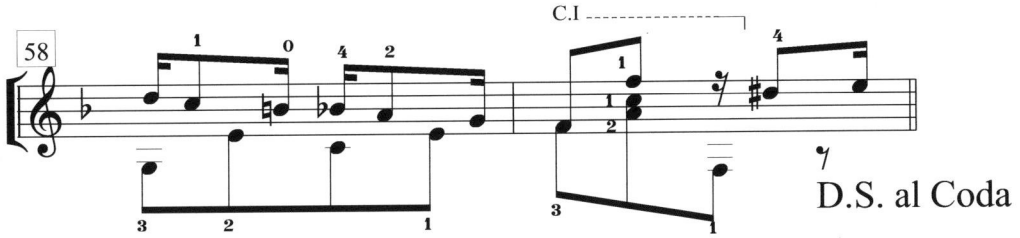

D.S. al Coda

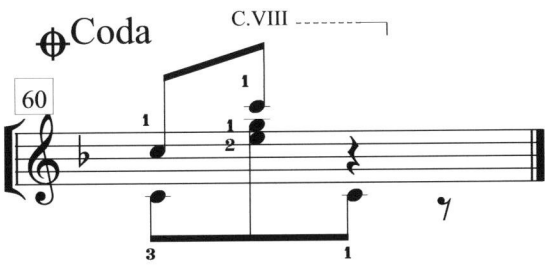

63

Gotas de ouro
(valsa)

Ernesto Nazareth
(arranged by Carlos Almada)

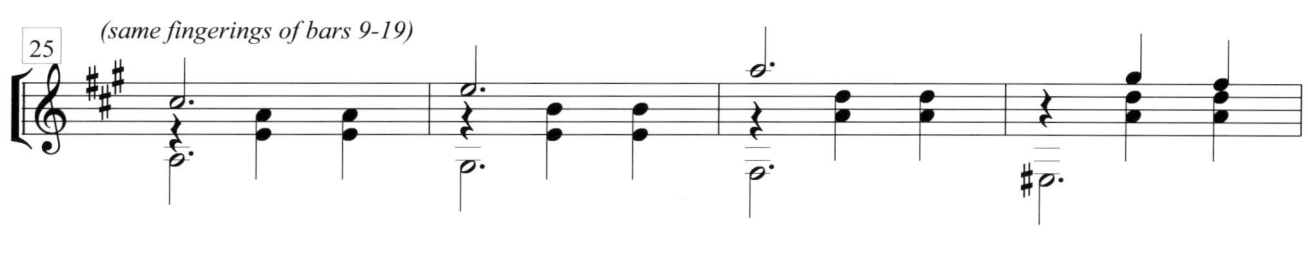

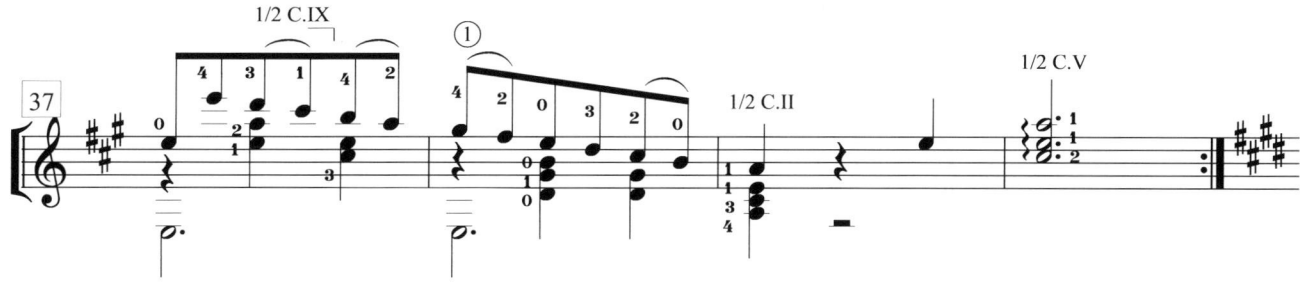
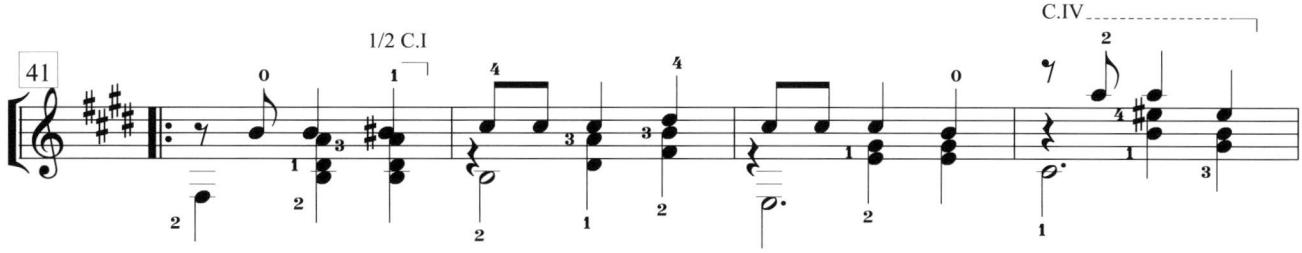
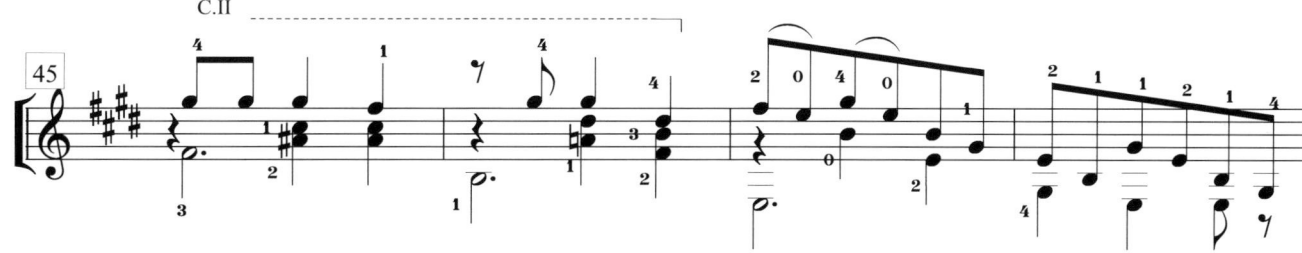

D.C. al Coda

Labirinto
(choro)

Ernesto Nazareth
(arranged by Flavio Henrique Medeiros)

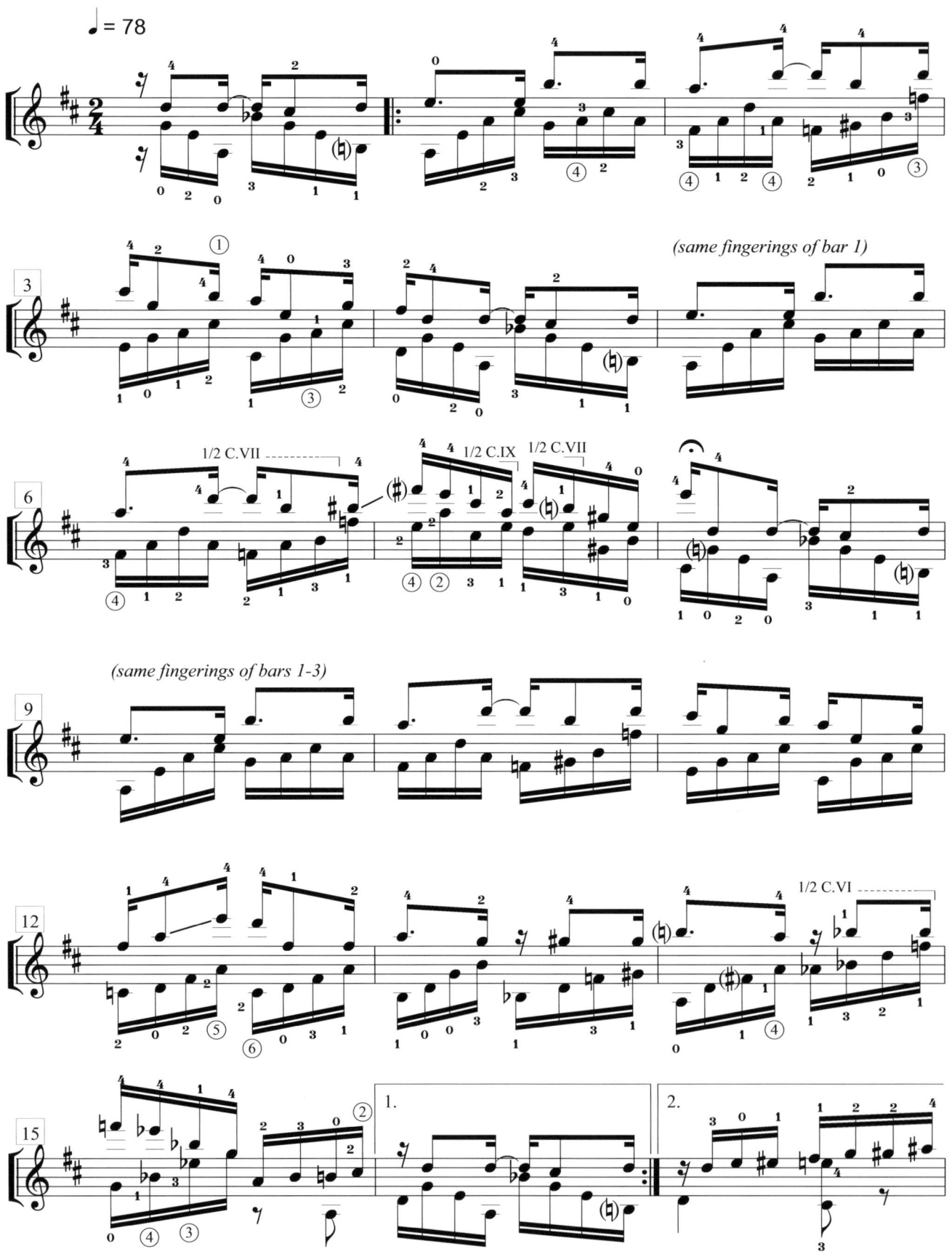

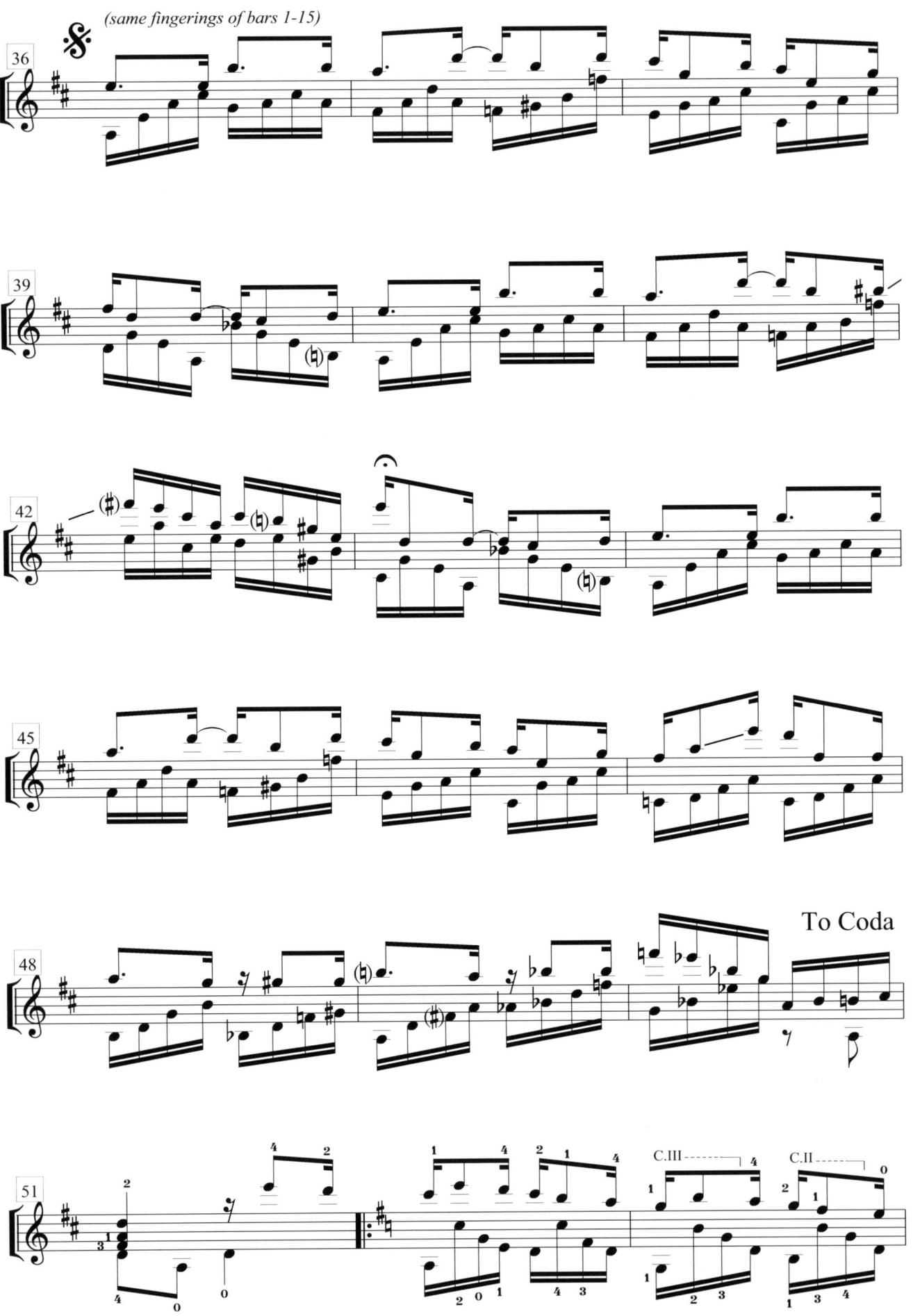

(same fingerings of bar 52)
C.VIII
54
C.VII
C.III
C.II
57
(same fingerings of bars 52-55)
60
1/2 C.VI
63
1/2 C.VII
66
D.S. al Coda
Coda
1/2 C.X
69

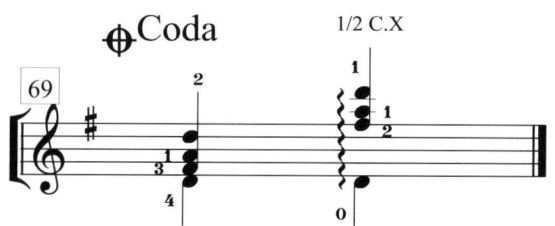

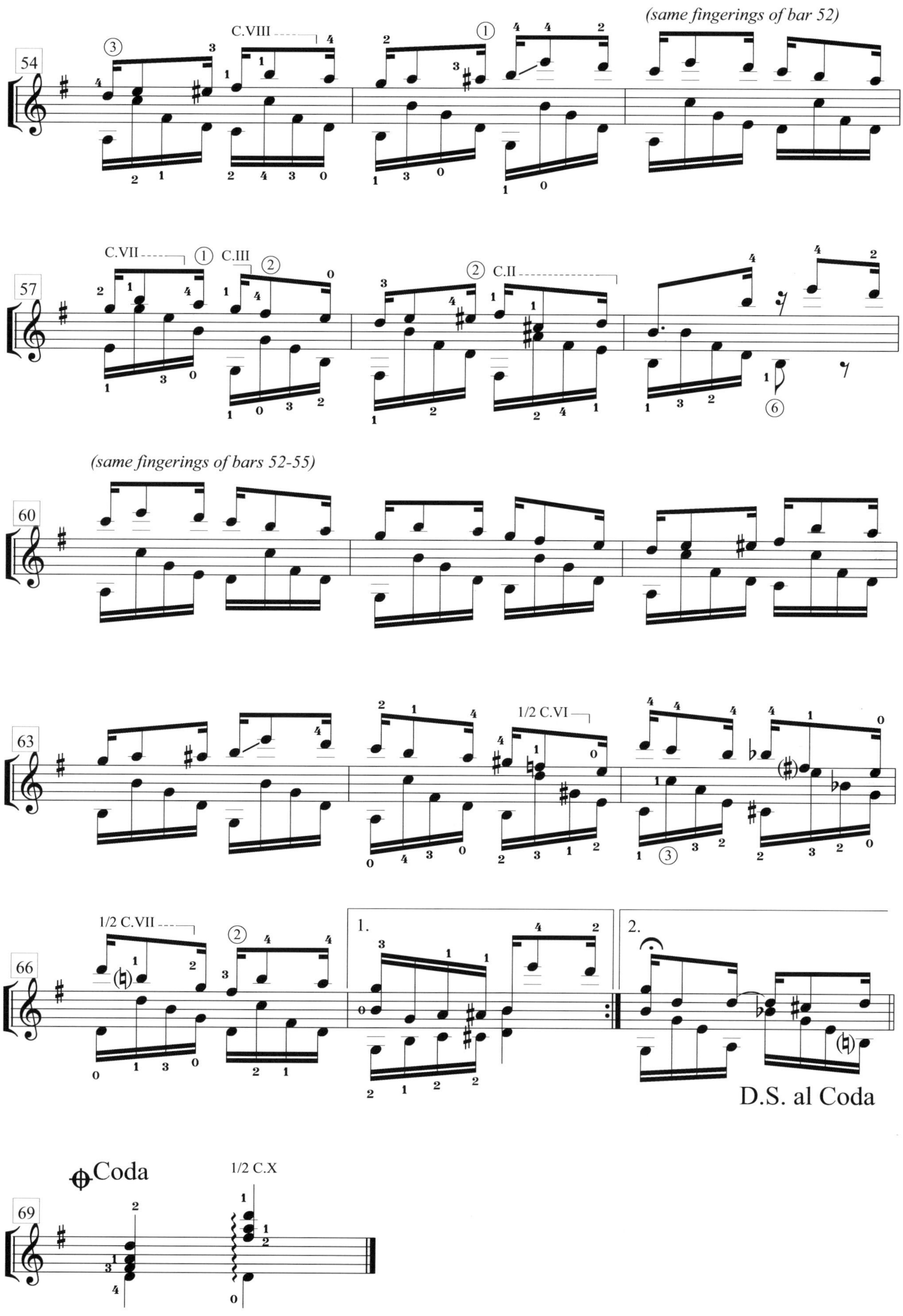

Matuto
(tango brasileiro)

Ernesto Nazareth
(arranged by Carlos Almada)

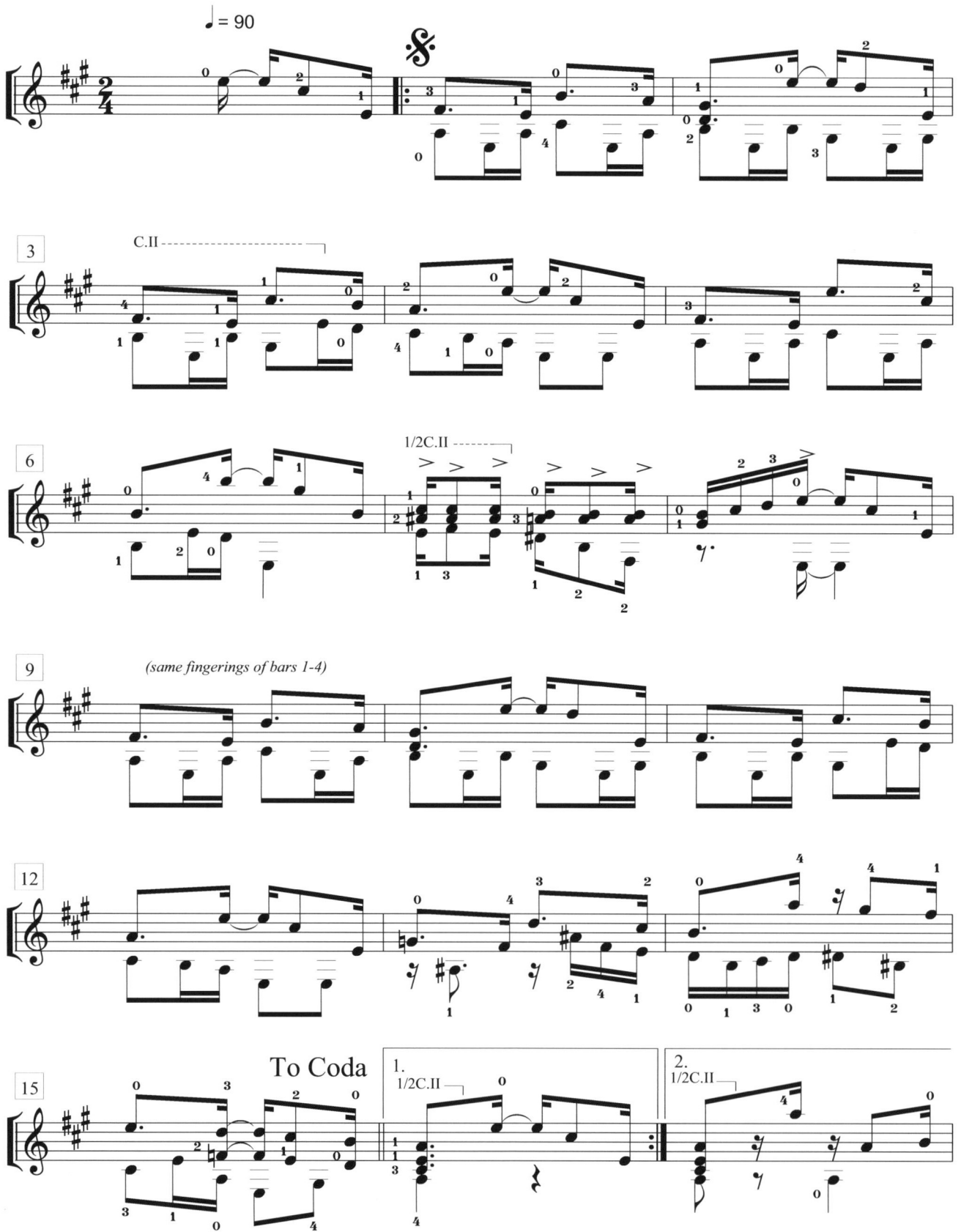

Nenê

(tango brasileiro)

Ernesto Nazareth
(arranged by Flavio Henrique Medeiros)

[6th = D]

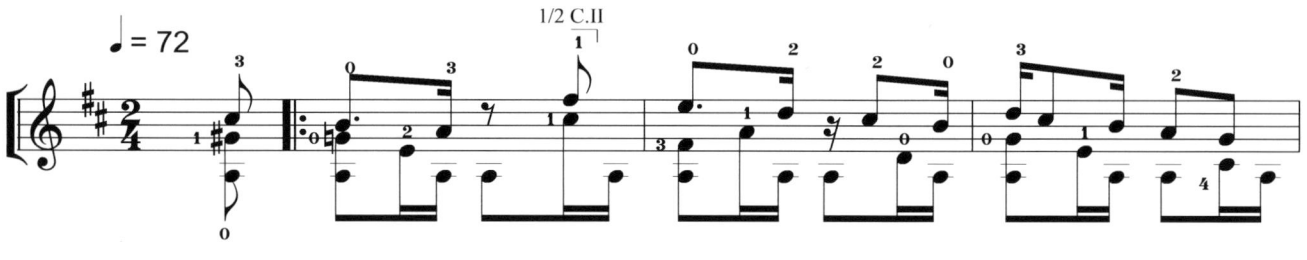

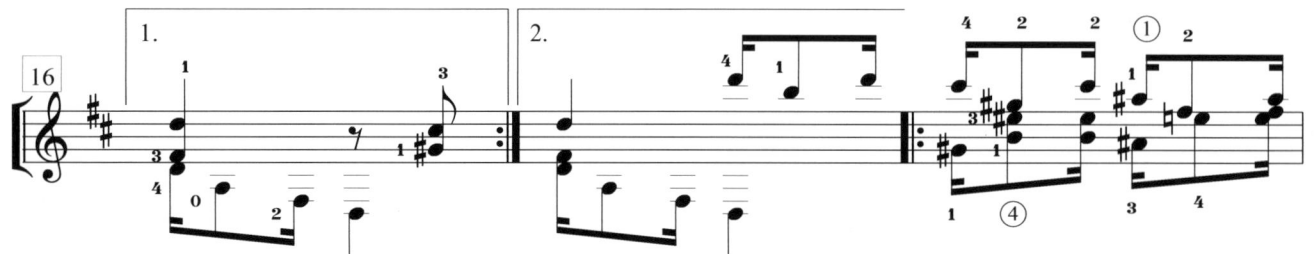

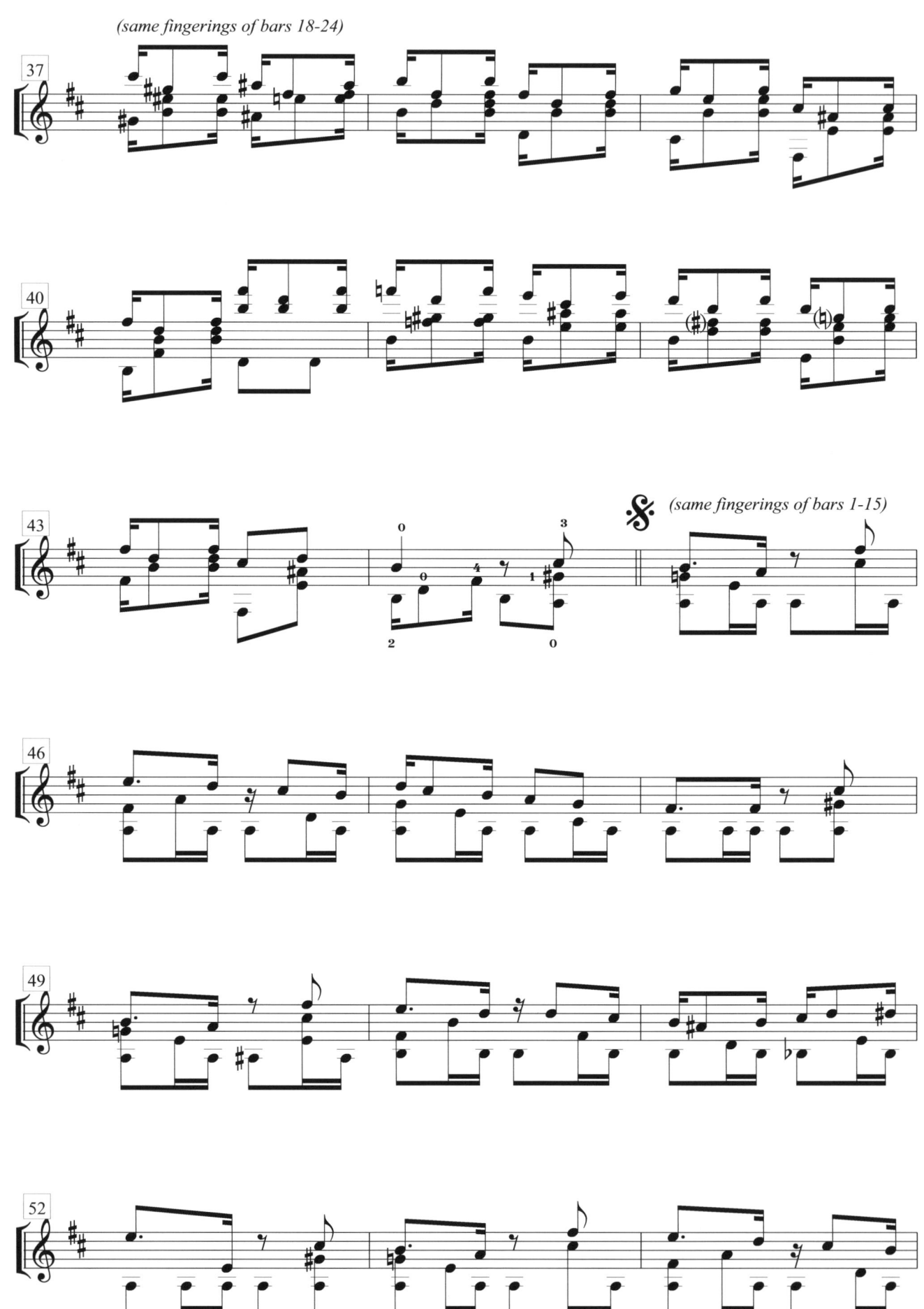

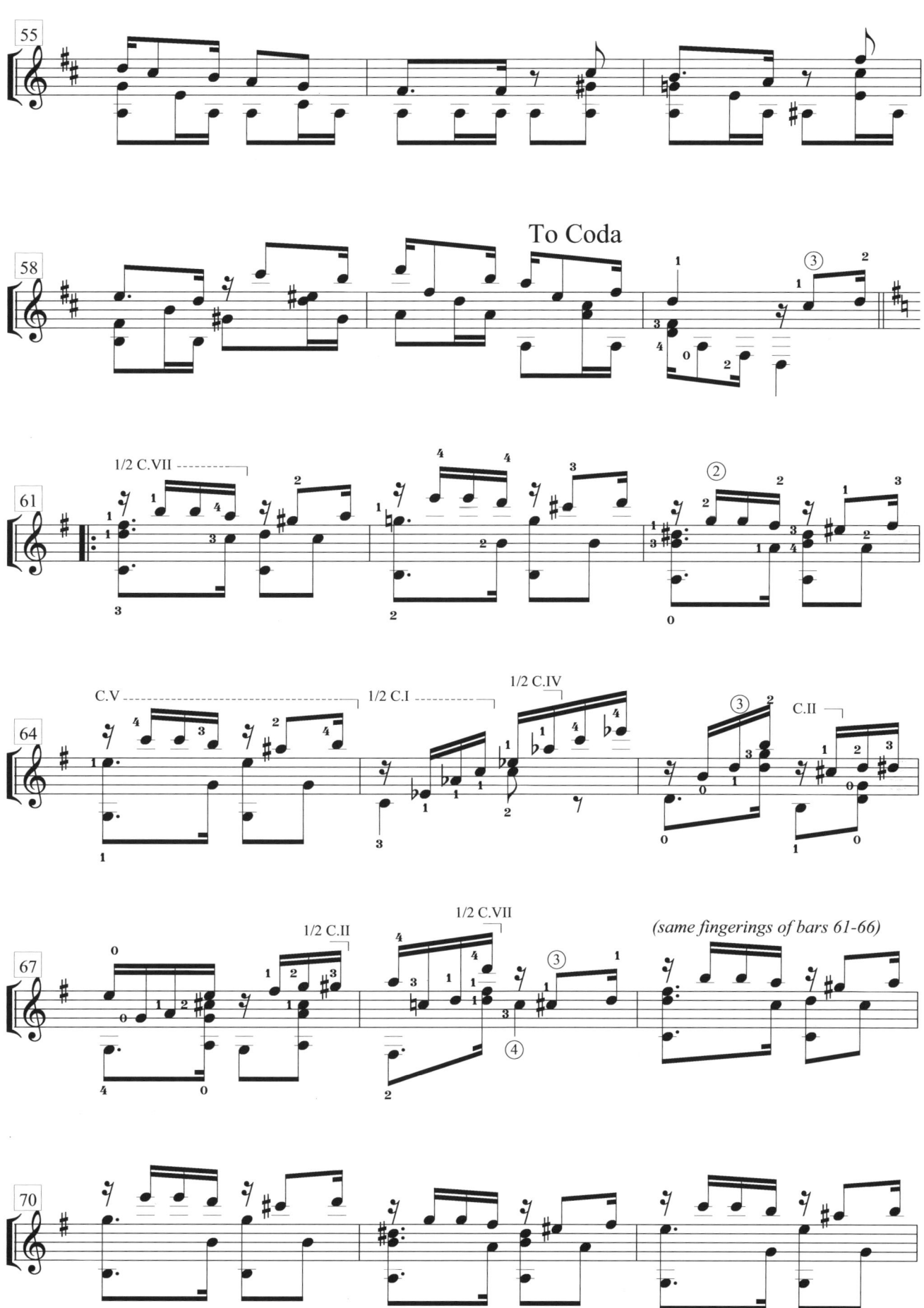

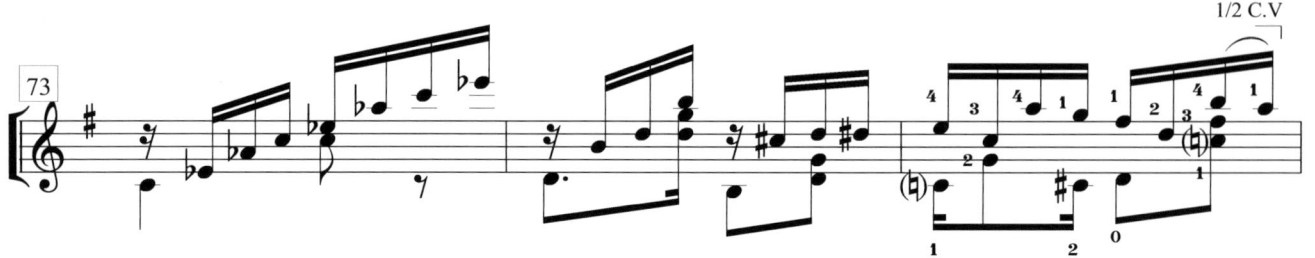
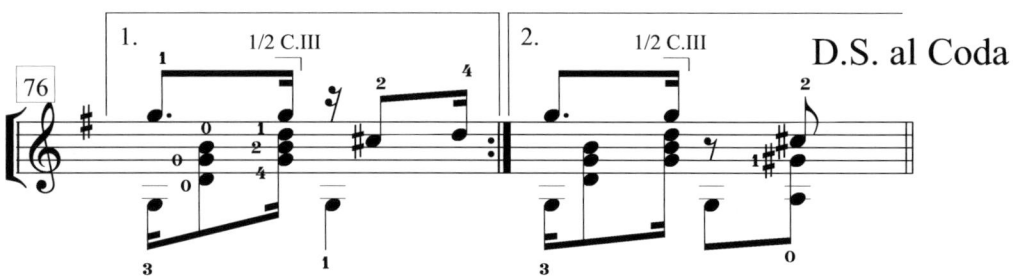
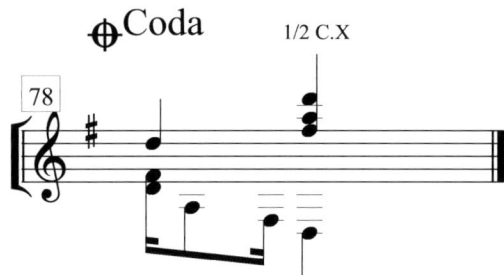

Nove de julho
(choro)

Ernesto Nazareth
(arranged by Carlos Almada)

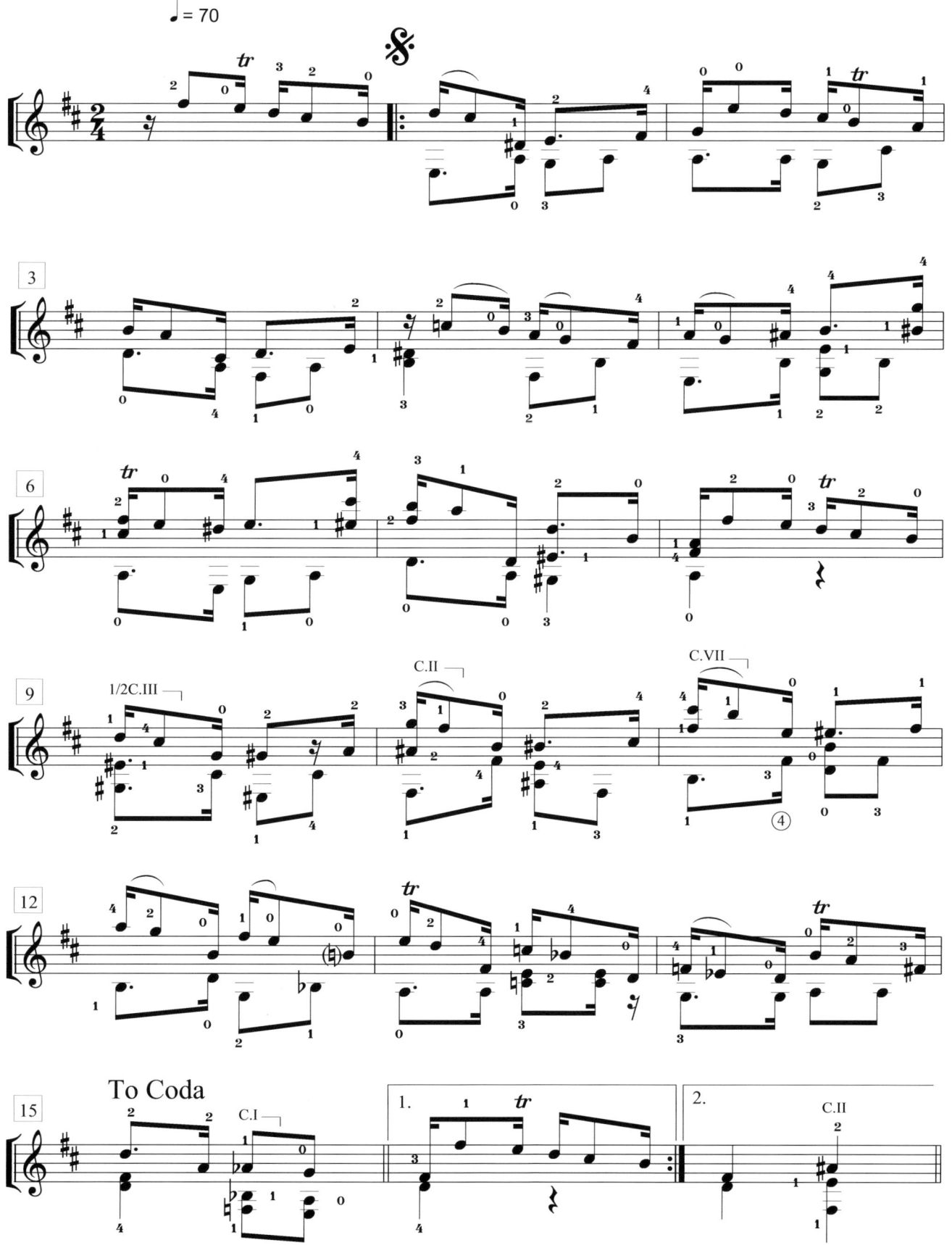

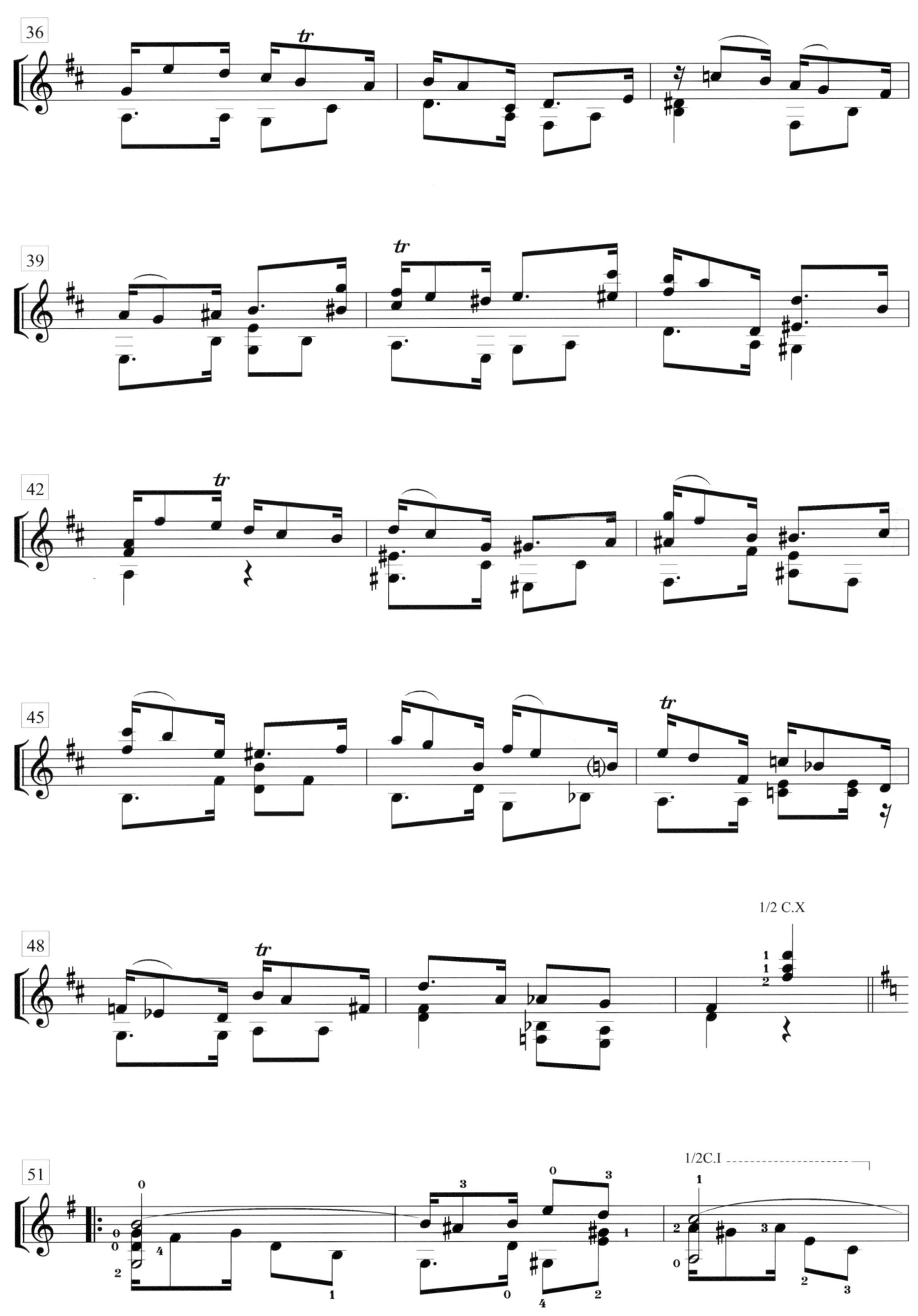

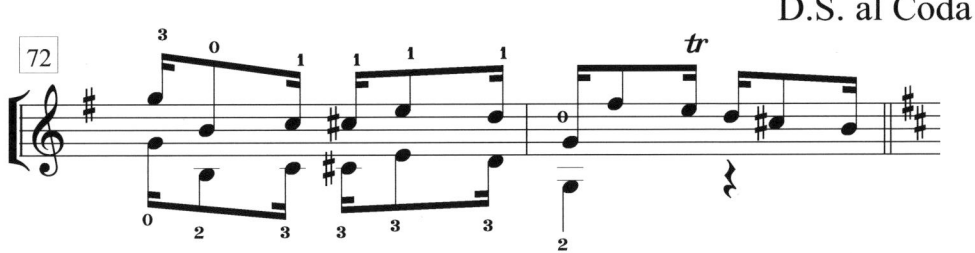

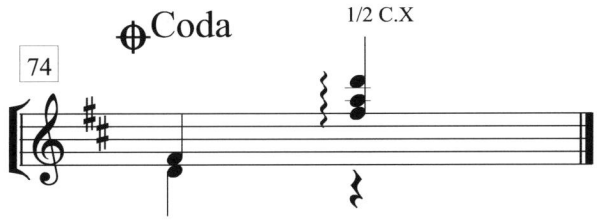

Odeon

(tango brasileiro)

Ernesto Nazareth
(arranged by Carlos Almada)

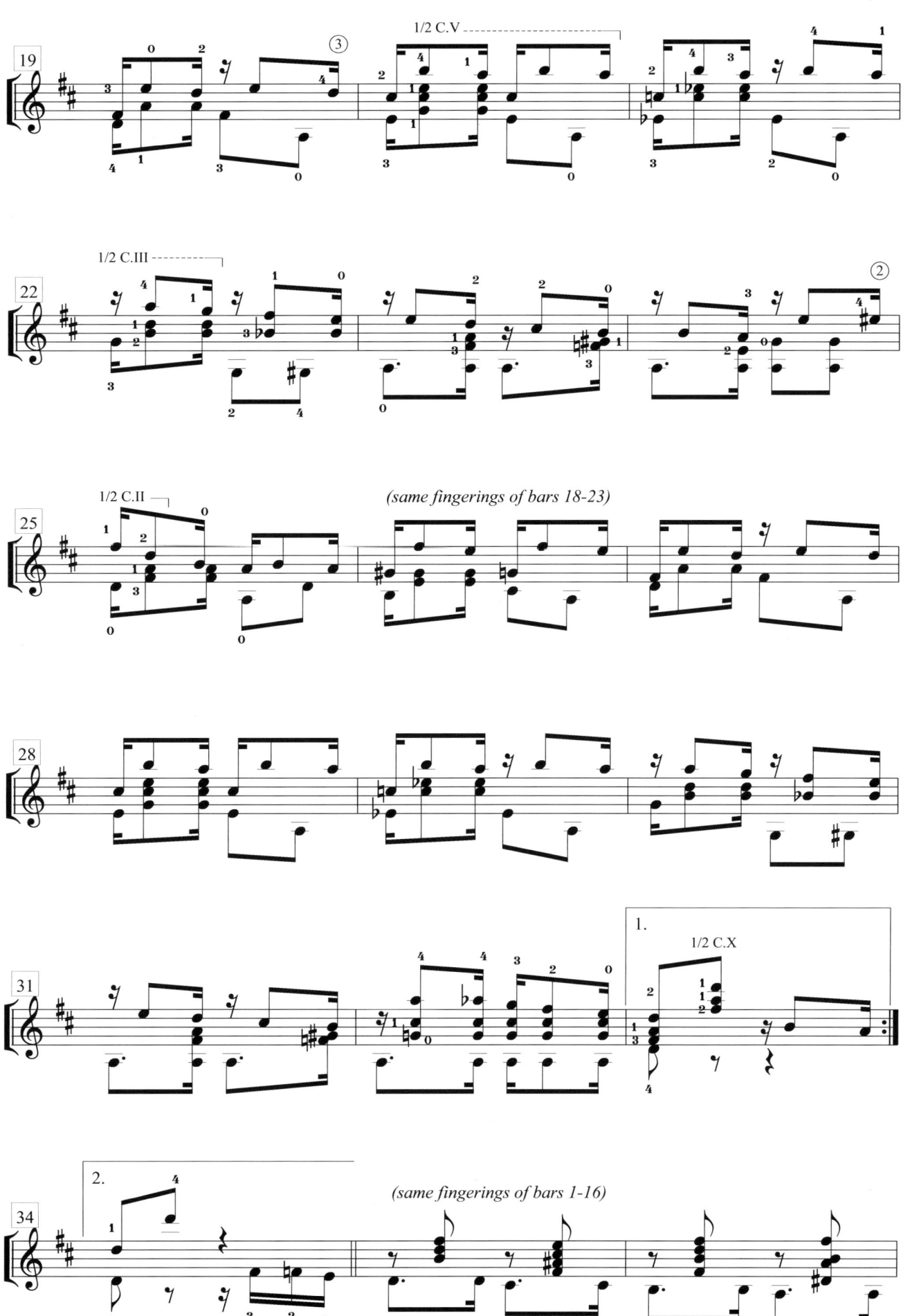

Pingüim

(tango brasileiro)

Ernesto Nazareth
(arranged by Flavio Henrique Medeiros)

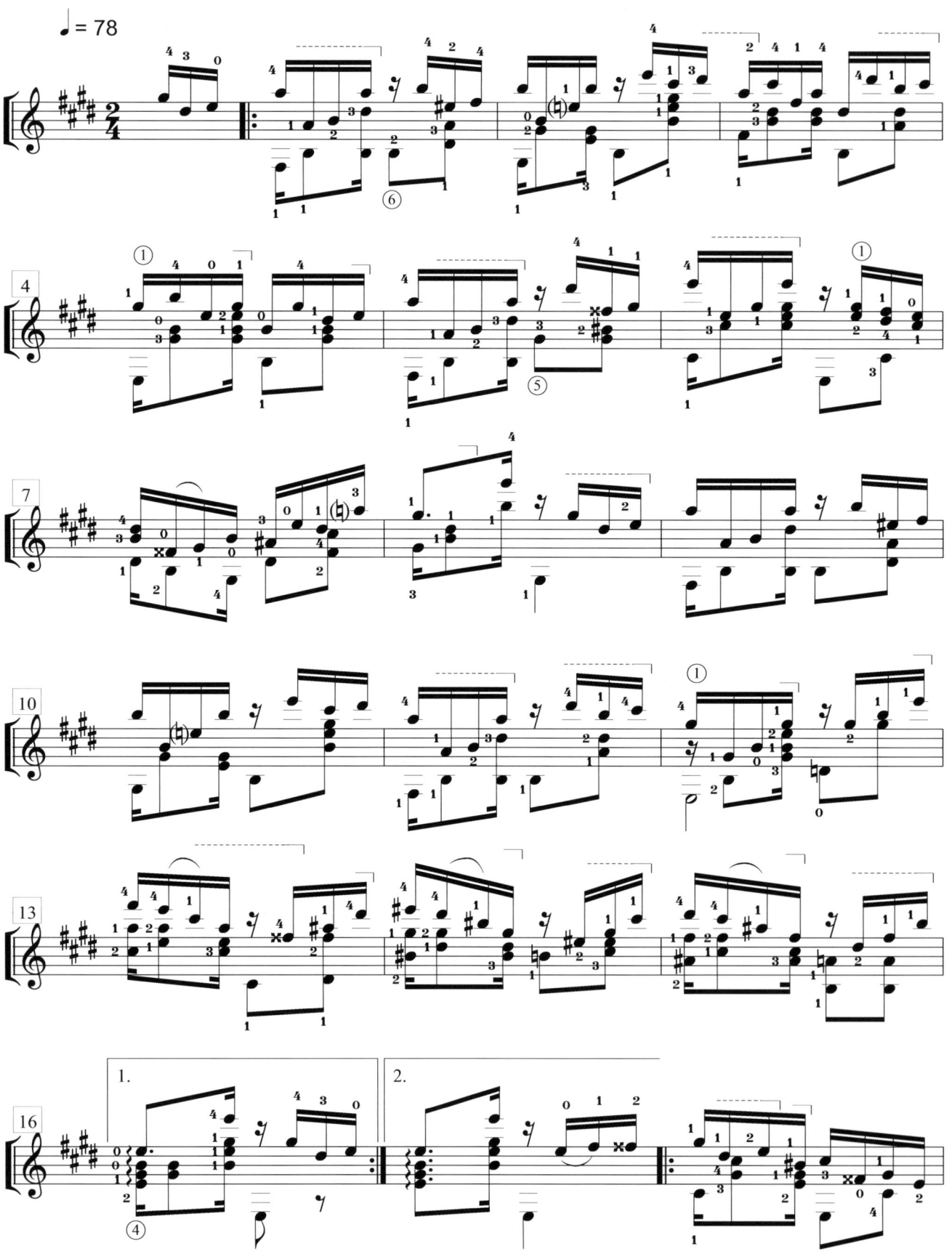

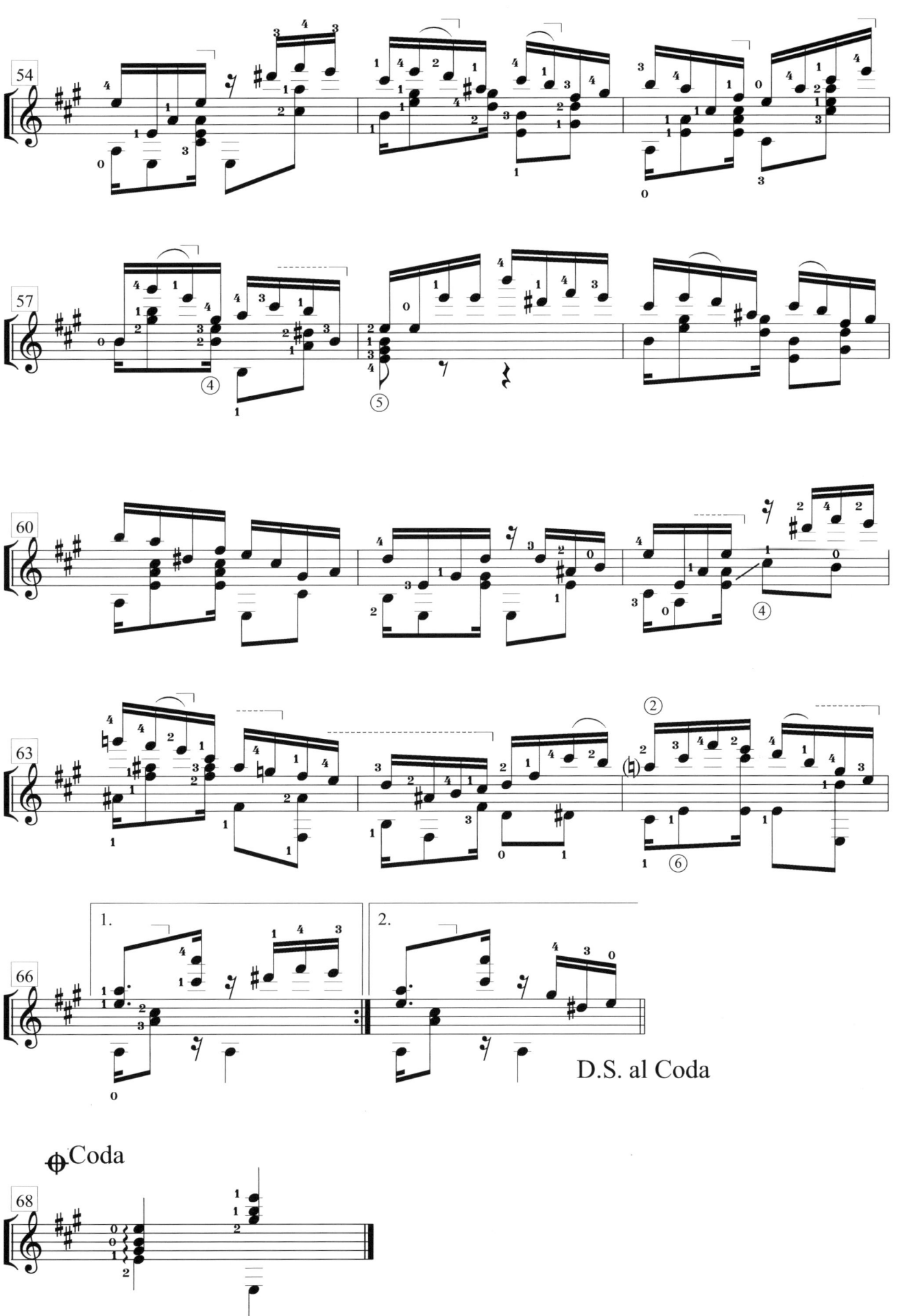

Quebradinha

(polca)

Ernesto Nazareth
(arranged by Carlos Almada)

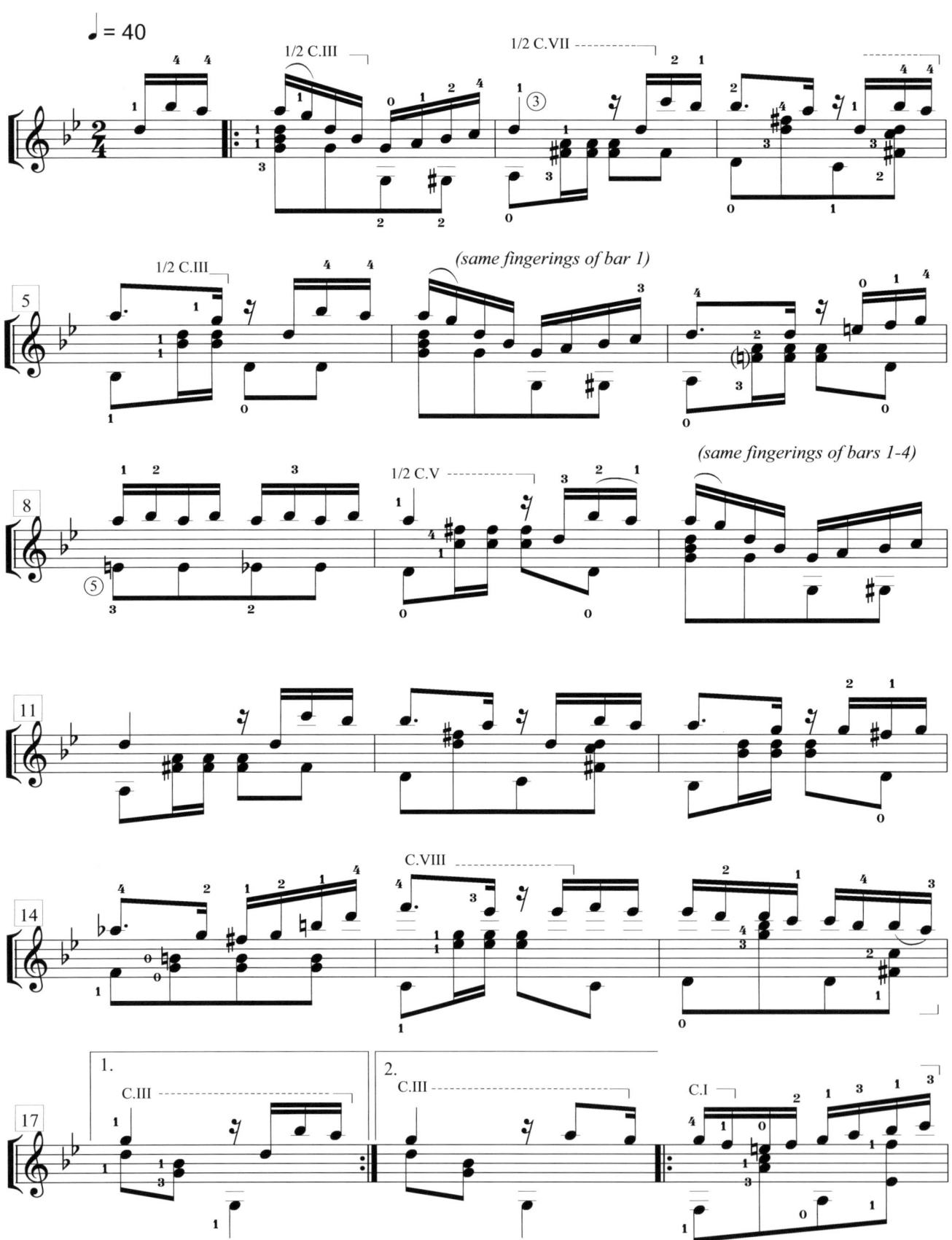

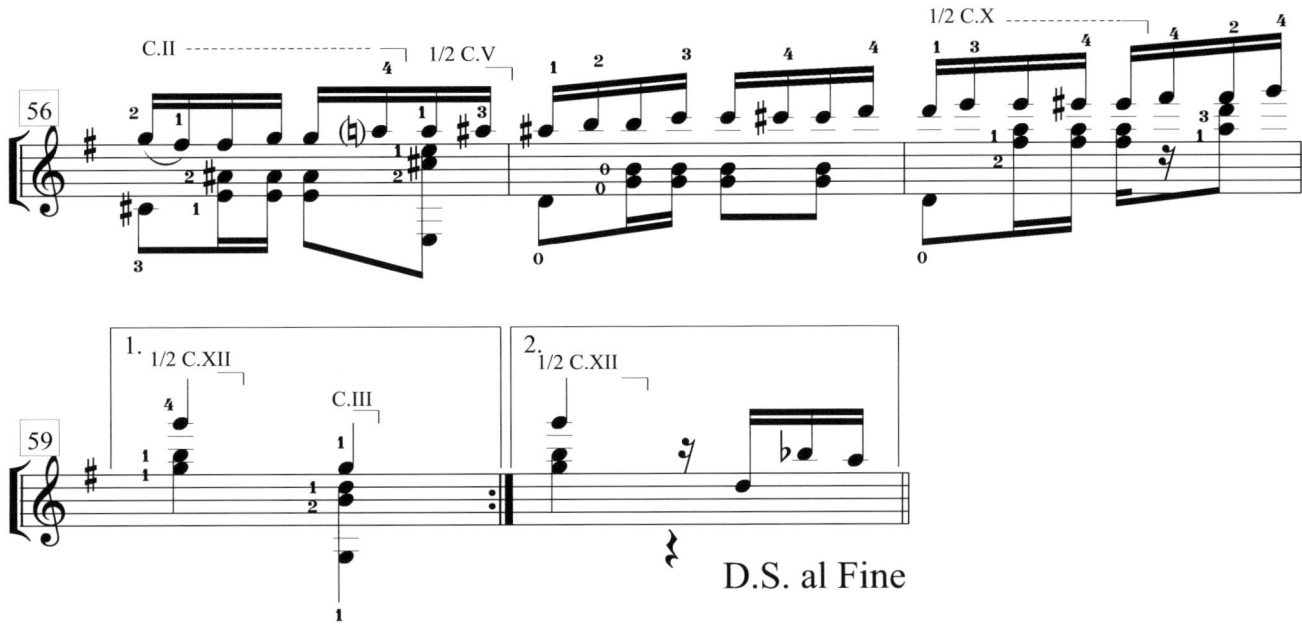

Rayon d'or
(polca-tango brasileiro)

Ernesto Nazareth
(arranged by Flavio Henrique Medeiros)

Sagaz

(tango brasileiro)

Ernesto Nazareth
(arranged by Carlos Almada)

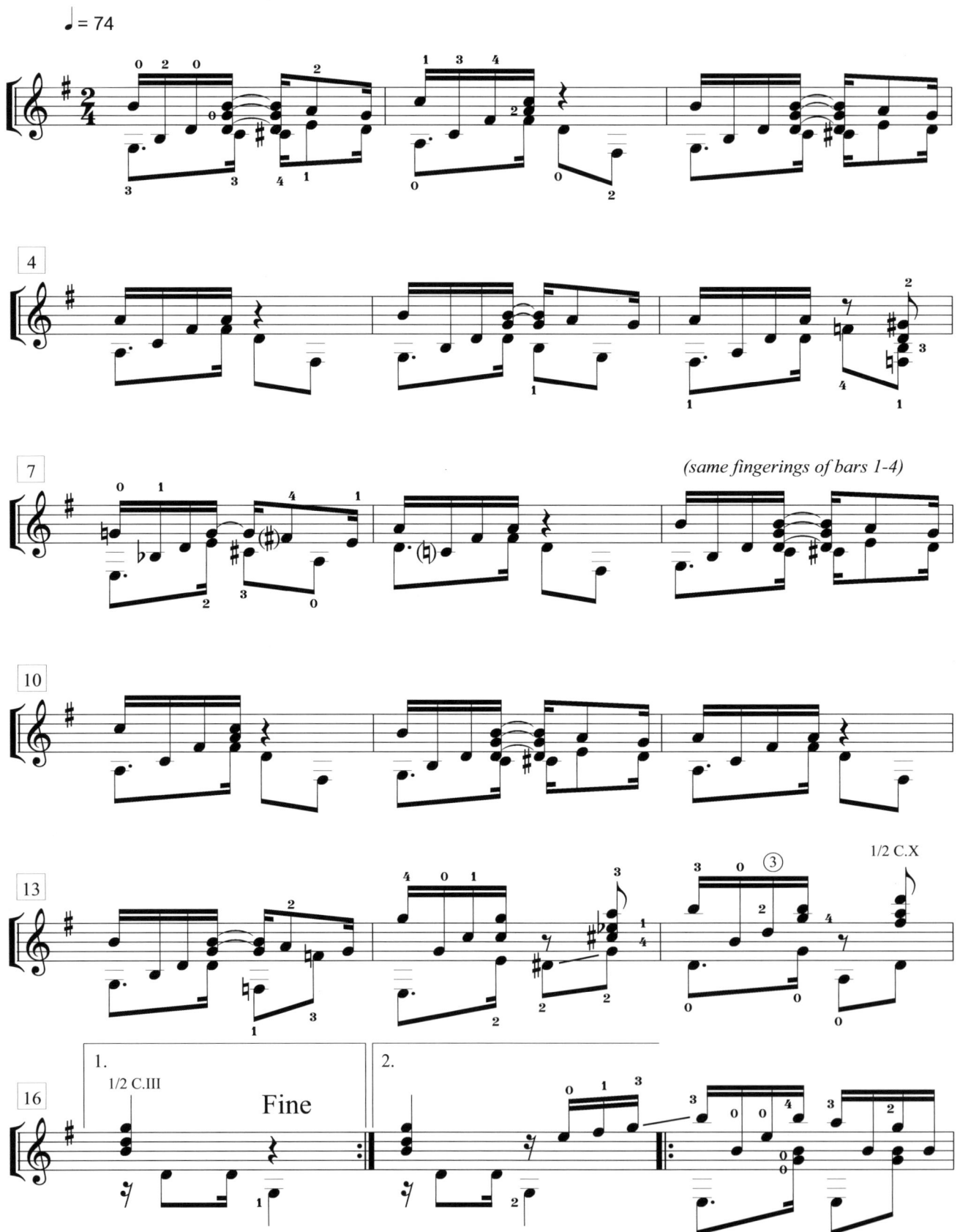

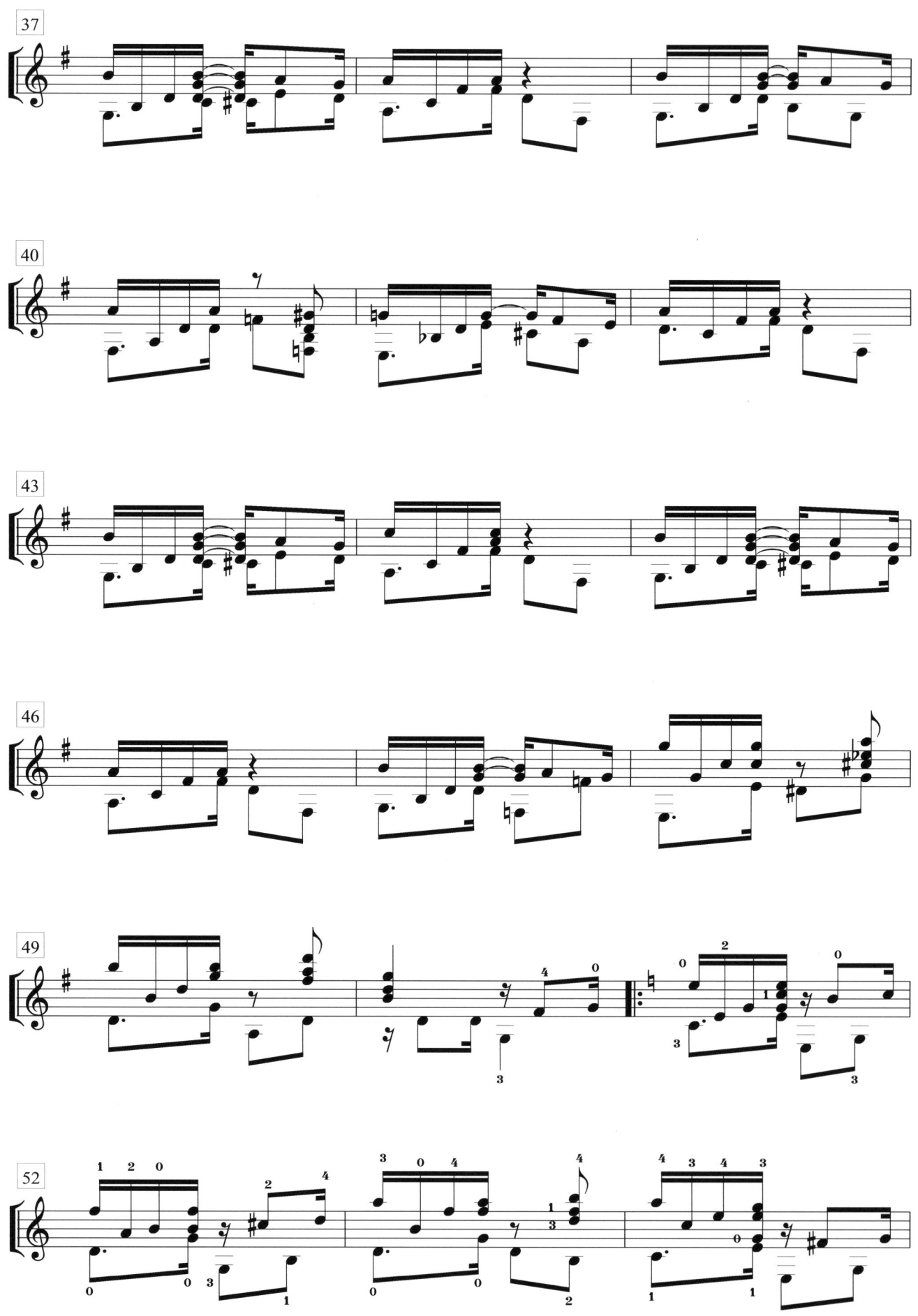

Sarambeque

(tango brasileiro)

Ernesto Nazareth
(arranged by Carlos Almada)

Saudade

(valsa)

Ernesto Nazareth
(arranged by Flavio Henrique Medeiros)

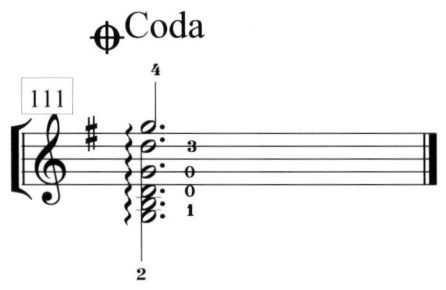

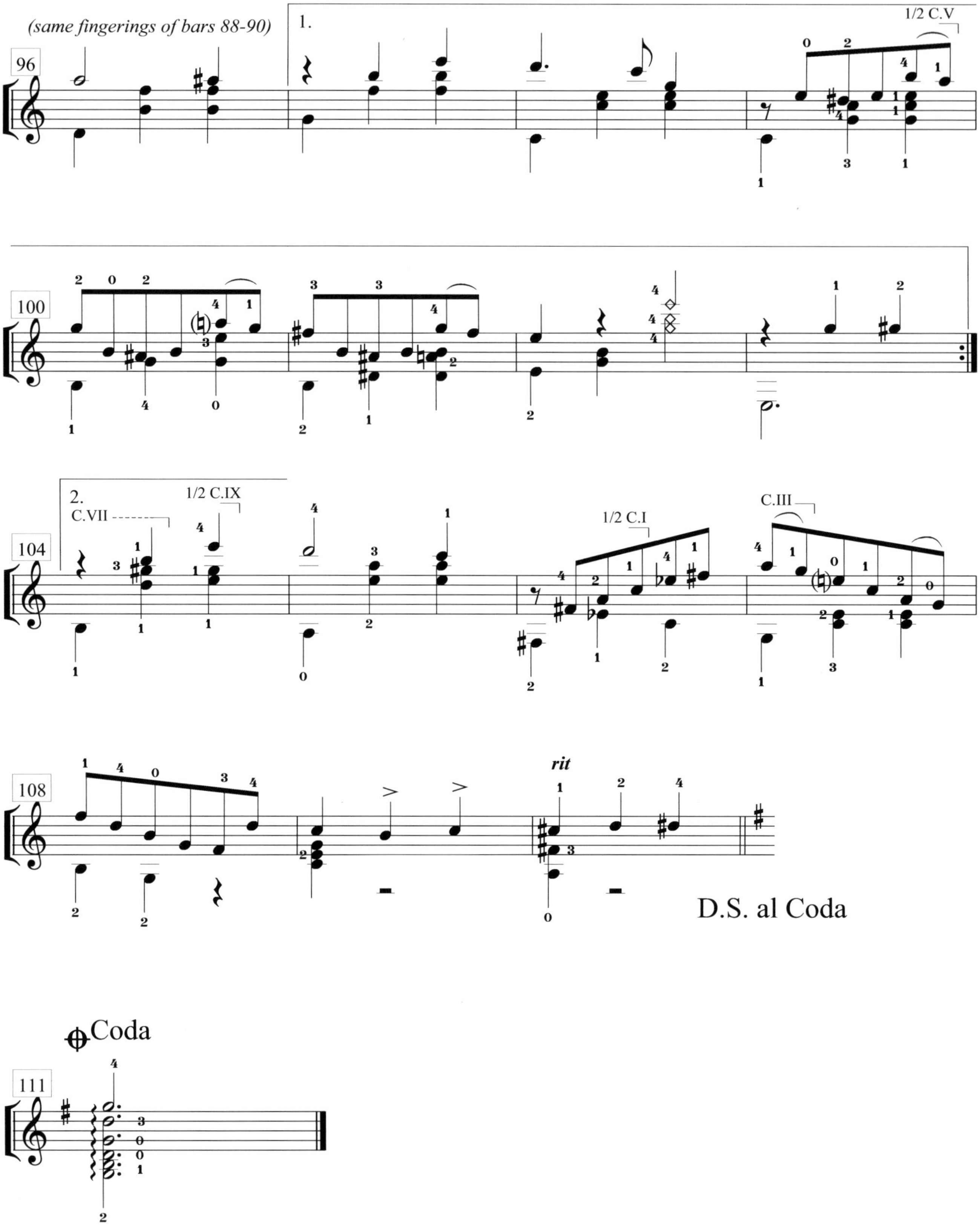

(same fingerings of bars 88-90)
96
1.
1/2 C.V
100
104
2.
C.VII
1/2 C.IX
1/2 C.I
C.III
108
rit
D.S. al Coda
Coda
111

This page has been left blank to avoid awkward page turns.

Tango Carnavalesco

(tango brasileiro)

Ernesto Nazareth
(arranged by Flavio Henrique Medeiros)

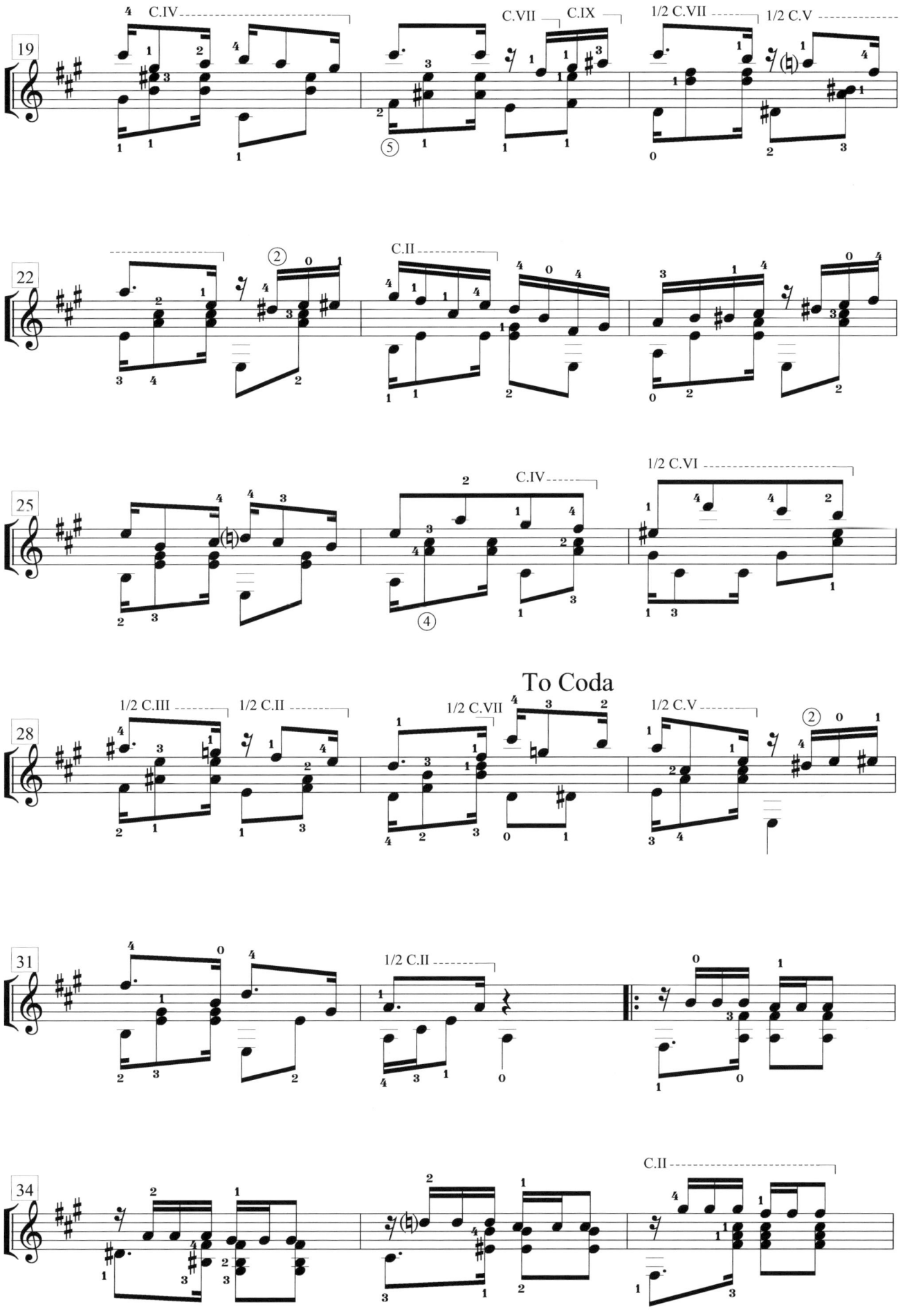

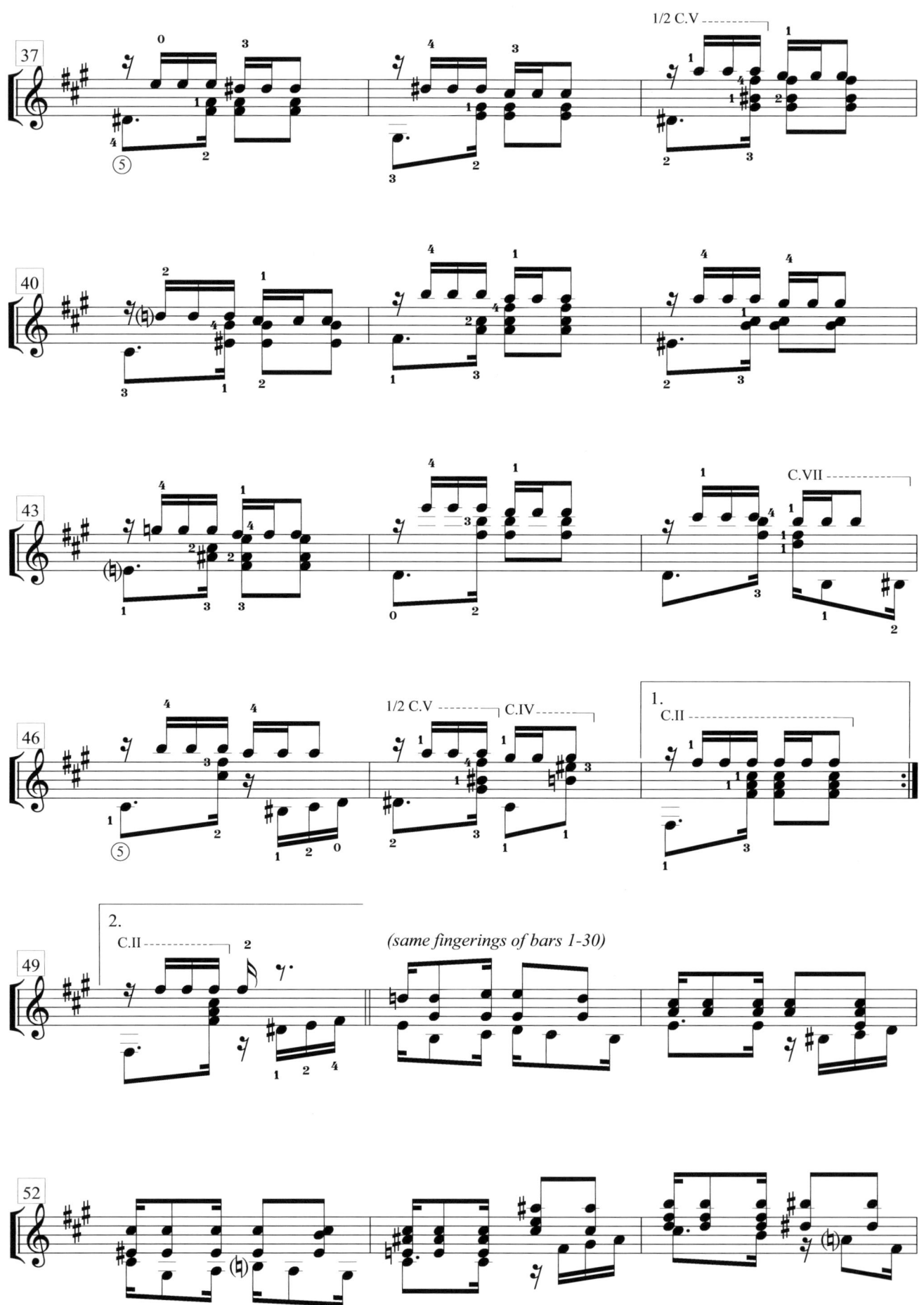

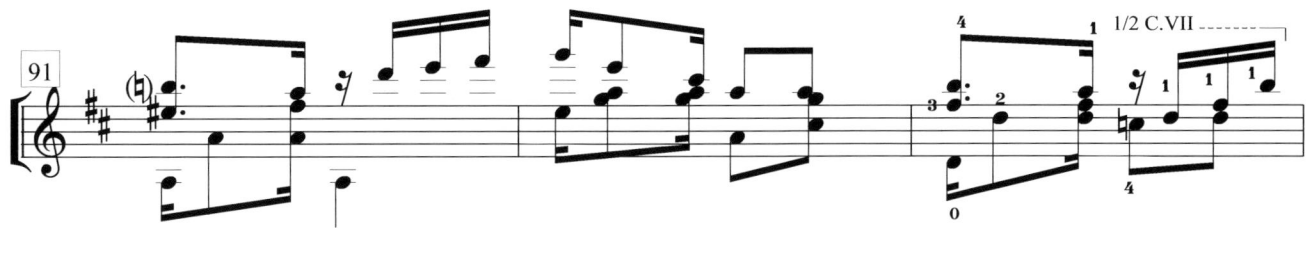

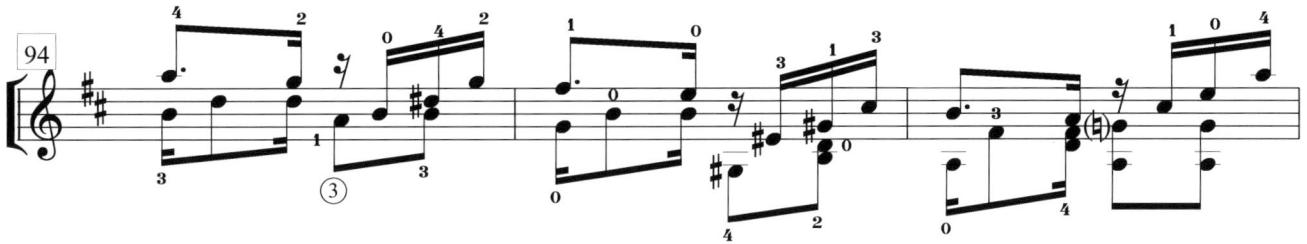

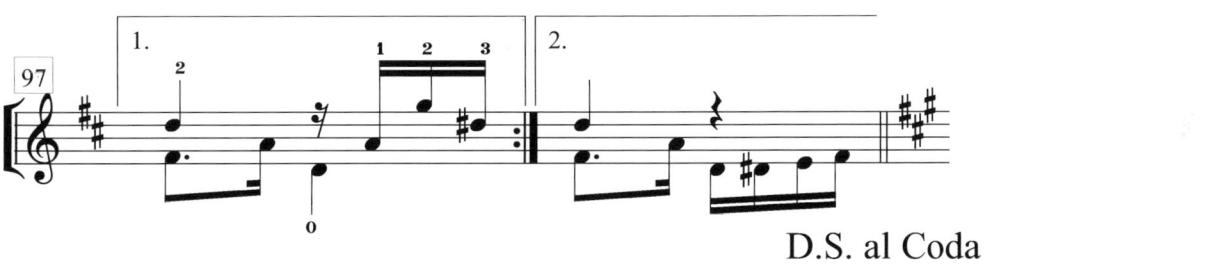

D.S. al Coda

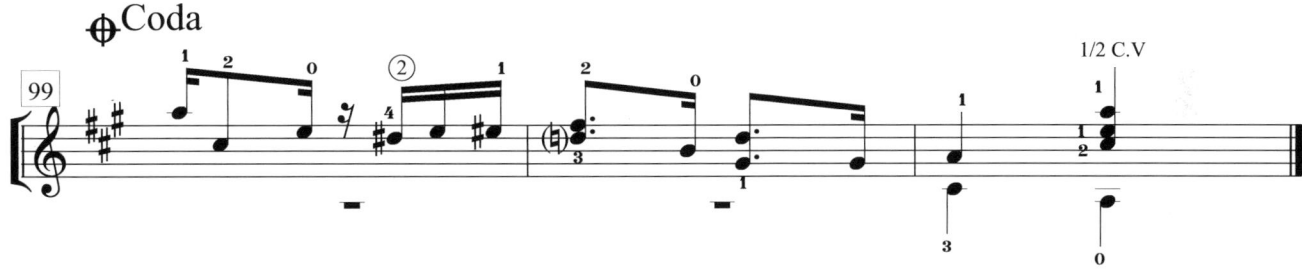

Tupinambá

(tango brasileiro)

Ernesto Nazareth
(arranged by Flavio Henrique Medeiros)

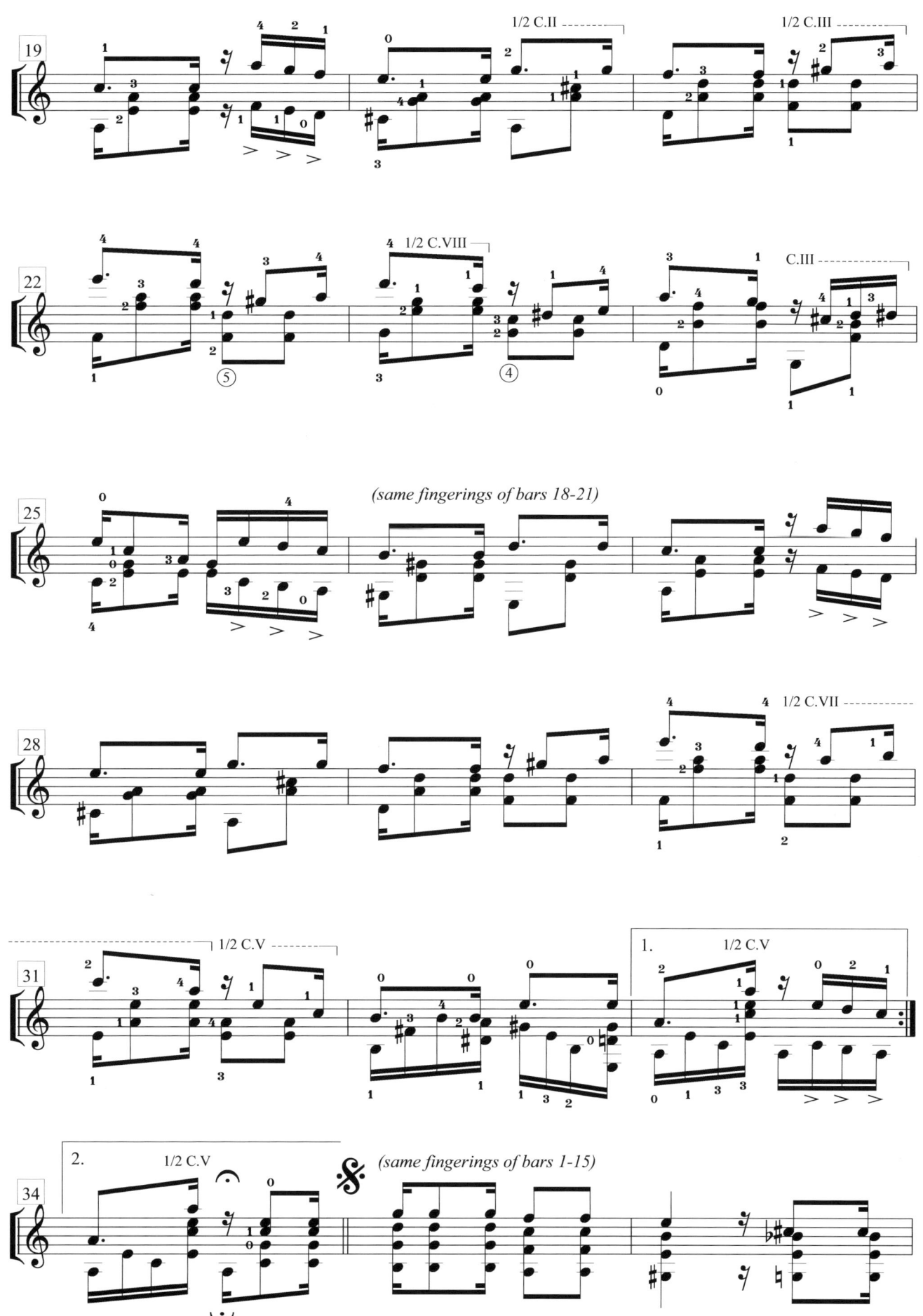

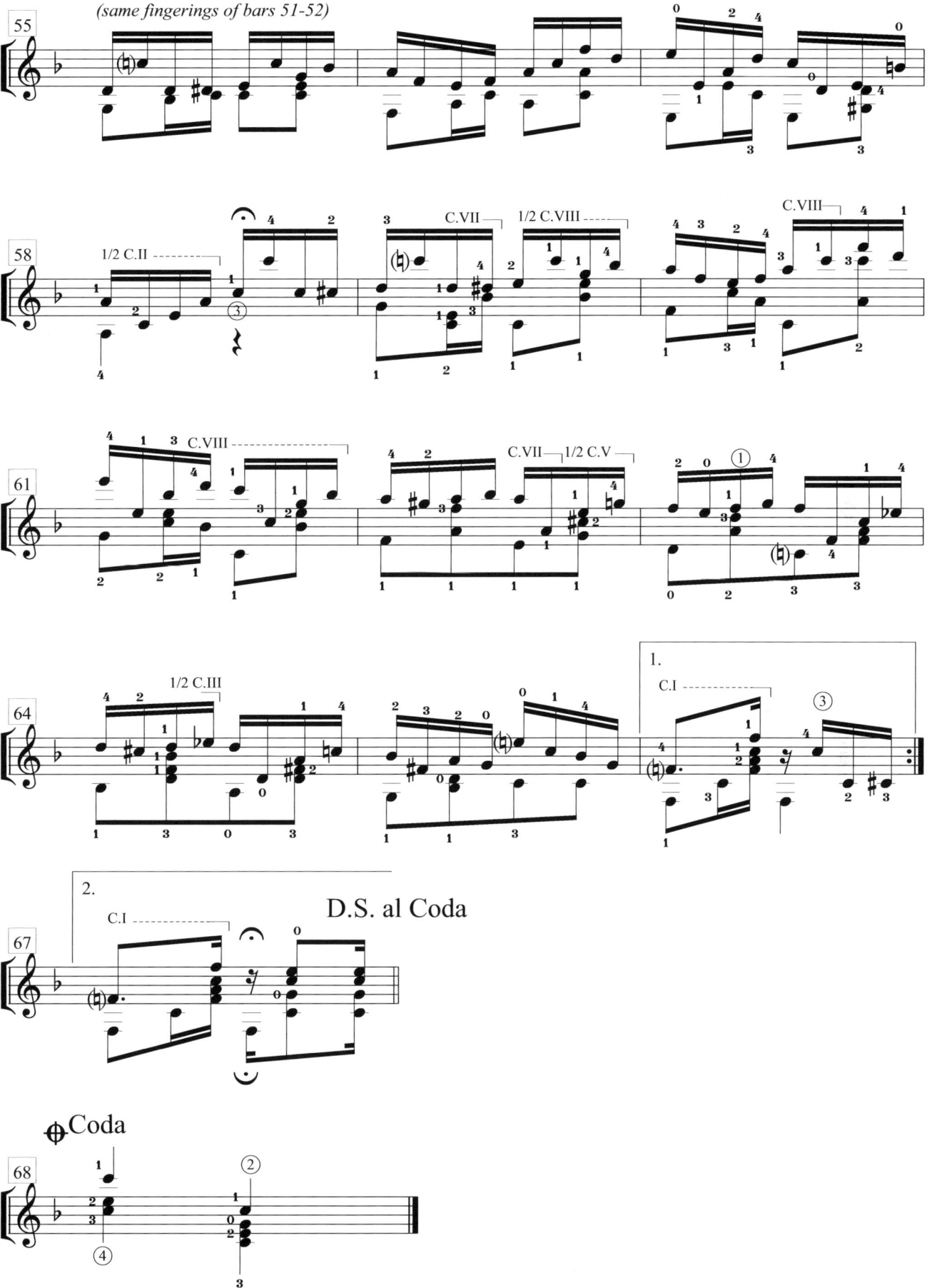

Vitorioso
(tango brasileiro)

Ernesto Nazareth
(arranged by Carlos Almada)

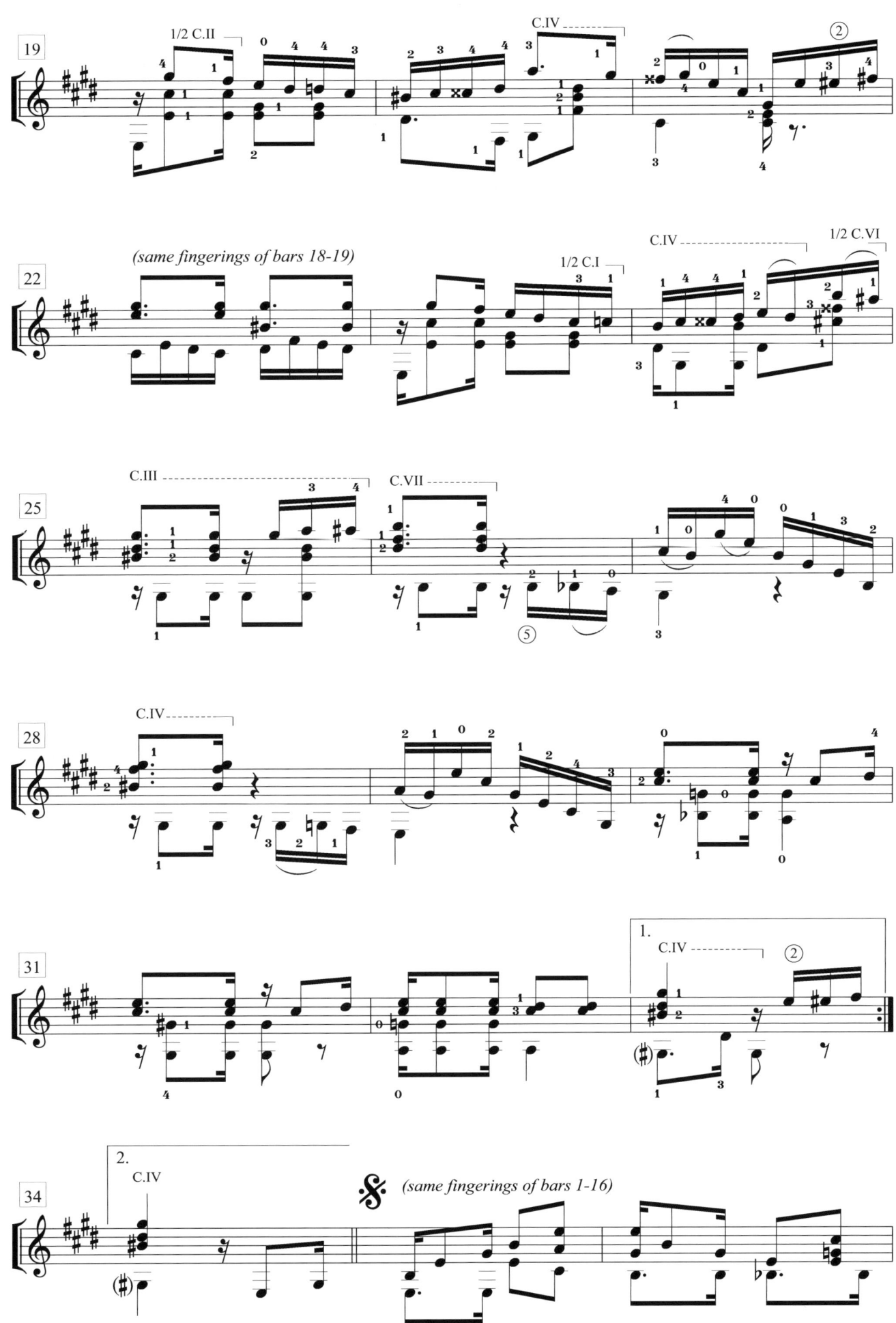

1922

(tango brasileiro)

Ernesto Nazareth
(arranged by Flavio Henrique Medeiros)

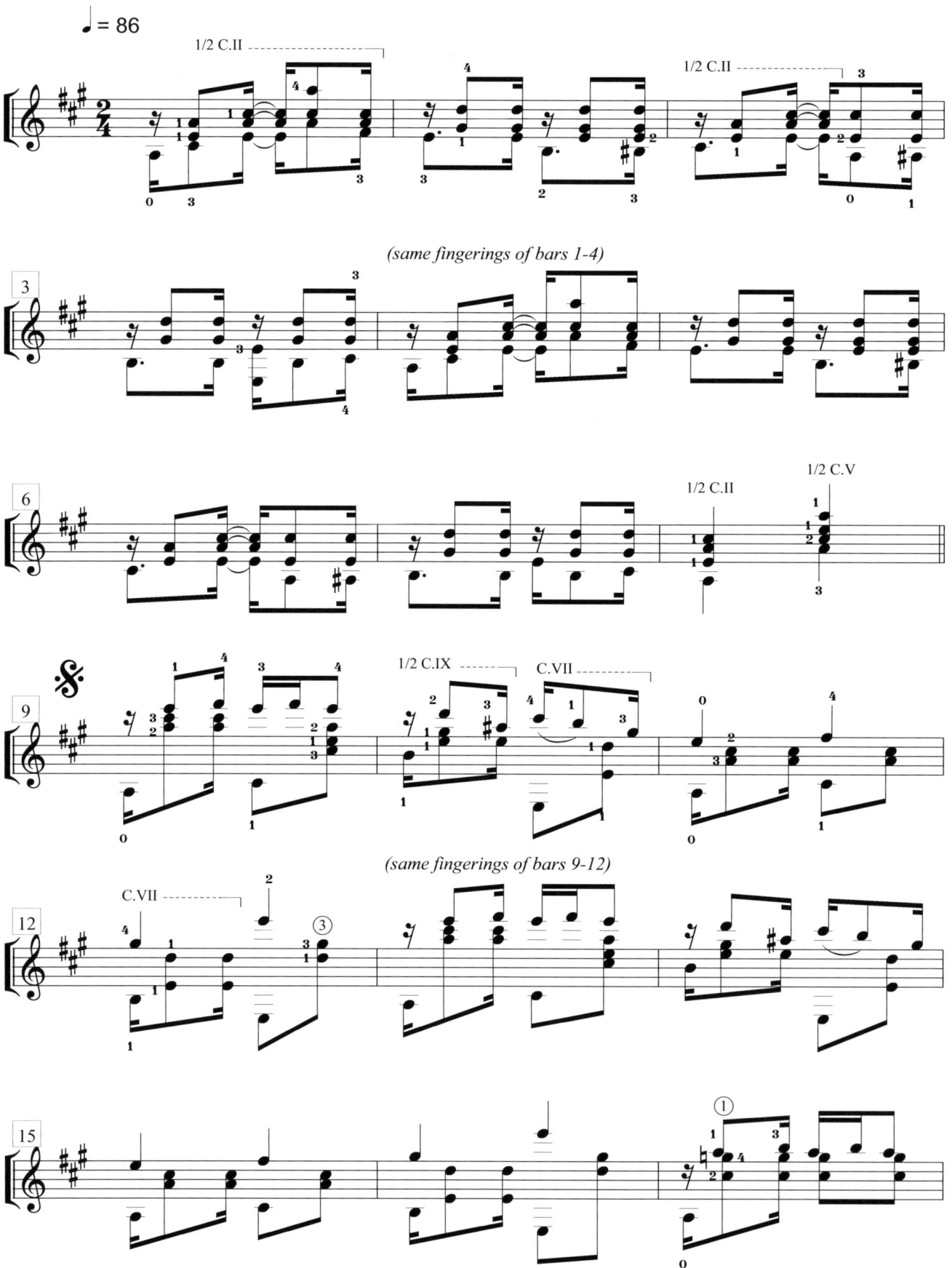

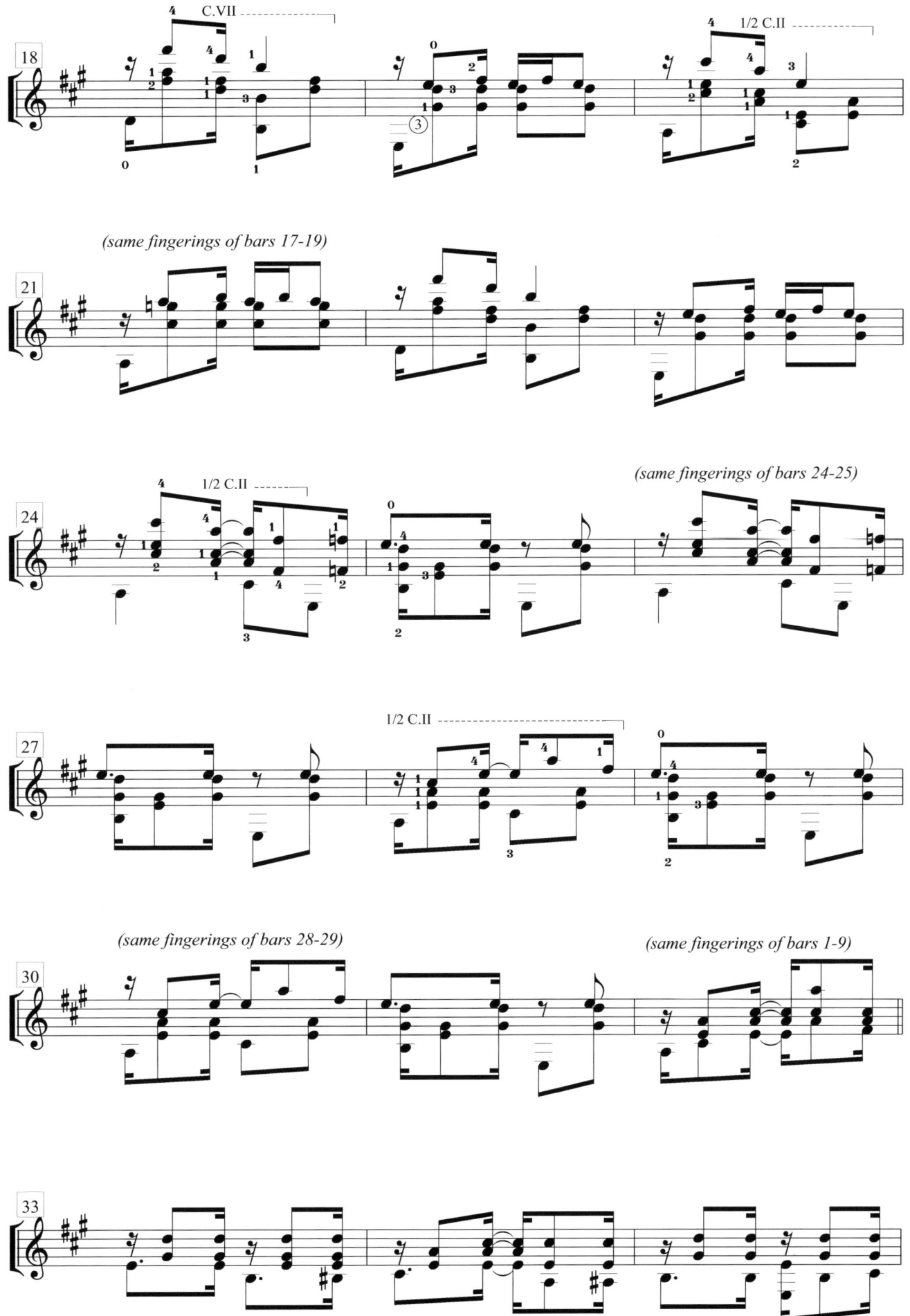

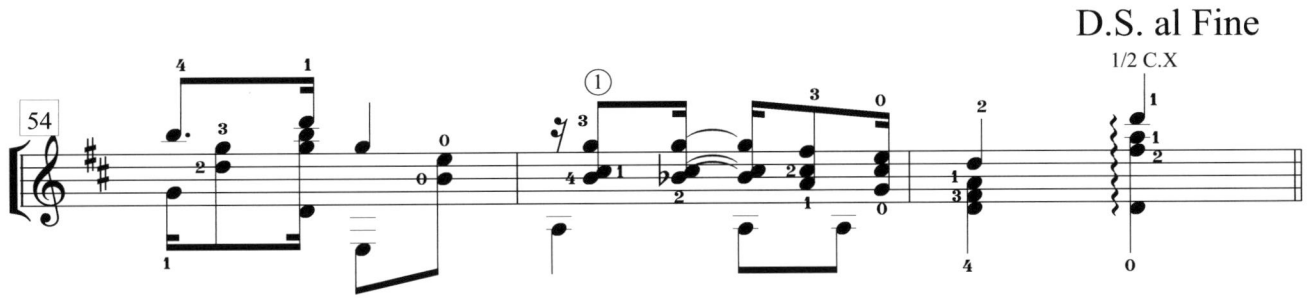

UNIQUELY INTERESTING MUSIC!